Instrument Pilot

ORAL EXAM GUIDE

MICHAEL D. HAYES

EIGHTH EDITION

THE COMPREHENSIVE GUIDE
TO PREPARE YOU FOR THE
FAA CHECKRIDE

Aviation Supplies & Academics, Inc.
Newcastle, Washington

Instrument Pilot Oral Exam Guide
Eighth Edition
by Michael D. Hayes

Aviation Supplies & Academics, Inc.
7005 132nd Place SE
Newcastle, Washington 98059-3153

Go to **www.asa2fly.com/reader/oegi** for further resources associated
with this book. Also, visit the ASA website often at **www.asa2fly.com/
TextbookUpdates** to find updates posted there due to FAA regulation
revisions that may affect this book.

Printed in the United States of America

2014   2013   9   8   7   6   5   4   3   2   1

ASA-OEG-I8
ISBN   978-1-61954-097-2

Library of Congress Cataloging-in-Publication Data:

Hayes, Michael D.
   Instrument oral exam guide : the comprehensive guide to prepare you for the FAA oral
exam / by Michael D. Hayes. — [New ed.]
      p.   cm.
   "ASA-OEG-I" — Cover.
   Includes bibliographical references.
   1. Instrument flying — Examinations, questions, etc.   2. Aeronautics — Examinations,
questions, etc.   3. United States. Federal Aviation Administration — Examinations, questions, etc. — Study guides. I. Title.
TL711.B6H39 1996   96-16988
629.132'5214'076—dc20   CIP

03

This guide is dedicated to the many talented students, pilots and flight instructors I have had the opportunity to work with over the years. Also, special thanks to Mark Hayes, Robert Hess, Meredyth Malocsay, and many others who supplied the patience, encouragement, and understanding necessary to complete the project.

— M.D.H.

Contents

Introduction

The *Instrument Oral Exam Guide* is a comprehensive guide designed for private or commercial pilots who are involved in training for the instrument rating. This guide was originally designed for use in a Part 141 flight school, but quickly became popular with those training under 14 CFR Part 61 not affiliated with an approved school. This book is also helpful for instrument-rated pilots who wish to refresh their knowledge or are preparing for an instrument proficiency check.

The guide is divided into four main sections which represent logical divisions of a typical instrument flight. In addition, a fifth section (Chapter 5) provides scenario-based questions which often test multiple subject areas. An FAA examiner may ask questions from any of the subject areas within these divisions, at any time during the practical test, to determine if the applicant has the required knowledge. Through intensive post-instrument-checkride debriefings, we have provided you with the most consistent questions asked along with the information necessary for a knowledgeable response.

One area often overlooked in the FAA practical test standards is the "Introduction" section, yet it contains very important information concerning the practical test. There are two specific subjects discussed within the PTS Introduction that deserve closer attention: "Special Emphasis Areas" and "Single-Pilot Resource Management." Special emphasis areas are aircraft operations that are considered critical to flight safety—the result of statistical analysis of accident investigation findings and pilot operational errors. The examiner will also evaluate the applicant's ability throughout the practical test to use good single-pilot resource management (SRM), which is comprised of six basic tenets: aeronautical decision making, risk management, task management, situational awareness, CFIT awareness, and automation management. Although these areas may not be specifically addressed under each task, they are essential to flight safety and will be critically evaluated during the practical test. Additional study material pertaining to these areas are provided by links on an ASA "Reader

Resource" webpage designed specifically for this Oral Exam Guide; these documents are available for download at the following address: **www.asa2fly.com/reader/oegi**.

At the end of this guide are three appendices. Appendix 1 has two checklists: the "Applicant's Practical Test Checklist," and the "Examiner's Practical Test Checklist" to be used when making final preparations for the instrument checkride. Appendix 2 contains the "Certified Flight Instructor—Instrument Airplane Supplement." This section provides additional study material for the CFII candidates preparing for the add-on to their existing CFI ticket. It also has study material of potential interest to all pilots preparing for the instrument checkride or an instrument proficiency check. Appendix 3 is an excerpt of the FAA's "Instrument Proficiency Check Guidance" document, a guide that assists a CFII in determining whether a pilot seeking an IPC endorsement has both the knowledge and skills for safe operation in all aspects of instrument flying. It should also prove very useful to pilots preparing for the instrument checkride or an instrument proficiency check—see a full version of this FAA guide on the "Reader Resource" webpage for this book.

You may supplement this guide with other study materials as noted in parentheses after each question; for example: (FAA-H-8083-15). The abbreviations for these materials and their titles are listed below. Be sure that you use the latest revision of these references when reviewing for the test. Also, check the ASA website at **www.asa2fly.com** for the latest updates to this book on our "Textbook Updates" page; all the latest changes in FAA procedures and regulations that affect these questions will be listed there.

14 CFR Part 43	*Maintenance, Preventive Maintenance, Rebuilding, and Alteration*
14 CFR Part 61	*Certification: Pilots, Flight Instructors, and Ground Instructors*
14 CFR Part 91	*General Operating and Flight Rules*
14 CFR Part 97	*Standard Instrument Procedures*
14 CFR Part 142	*Training Centers*
AC 00-6	*Aviation Weather*
AC 00-45	*Aviation Weather Services*
AIM	*Aeronautical Information Manual*

FAA-H-8083-2	*Risk Management Handbook*
FAA-H-8083-3	*Airplane Flying Handbook*
FAA-H-8083-6	*Advanced Avionics Handbook*
FAA-H-8083-9	*Aviation Instructor's Handbook*
FAA-H-8083-15	*Instrument Flying Handbook*
FAA-H-8083-25	*Pilot's Handbook of Aeronautical Knowledge*
FAA-H-8083-30	*Aviation Maintenance Technician Handbook—General*
FAA-H-8261-1	*Instrument Procedures Handbook*
FAA-S-8081-4	*Instrument Rating Practical Test Standards*
P/CG	*Pilot/Controller Glossary included in the AIM*
USRGD	*FAA Aeronautical Chart User's Guide*

All the books listed above are reprinted by ASA and are available from aviation retailers worldwide.

14 CFR Part 93	*Special Air Traffic Rules*
14 CFR Part 95	*IFR Altitudes*
AC 00-54	*Pilot Windshear Guide*
AC 61-65	*Certification: Pilots, and Flight Instructors, and Ground Instructors*
AC 61-67	*Stall and Spin Awareness Training*
AC 61-98	*Currency and Additional Qualification Requirements for Certificated Pilots*
AC 90-100	*U.S. Terminal and En Route Area Navigation (RNAV) Operations*
AC 90-107	*Guidance for Localizer Performance with Vertical Guidance and Localizer Performance without Vertical Guidance Approach Operations in the U.S. National Airspace System*
AC 91-51	*Effect of Icing on Aircraft Control and Airplane Deice and Anti-Ice Systems*
AC 91-73	*Parts 91 and 135 Single Pilot, Flight School Procedures During Taxi Operations*
AC 91-74	*Pilot Guide: Flight in Icing Conditions*

Continued

AC 91-78	*Use of Class 1 or Class 2 Electronic Flight Bag (EFB)*
A/FD	*Airport/Facility Directory*
FAA-P-8740-16	*Understanding and Caring for your Gyroscopic Instruments*
Order 8260.3B	*United States Standard for Terminal Instrument Procedures (TERPs)*
POH	*Pilot Operating Handbook*
AFM	*FAA Approved Flight Manual*

These FAA materials are available from the Government Printing Office or at www.faa.gov. POH/AFMs are available from the airplane manufacturer.

A review of the information presented within this guide should provide the necessary preparation for the oral section of an FAA instrument certification or re-certification check.

Were you asked a question during your checkride that was not covered in this book? If so, please send the question to ASA. We are constantly striving to improve our publications to meet the industry needs.

email: asa@asa2fly.com
Fax: 425.235.0128

7005 132nd Place SE
Newcastle, WA 98059-3153

Preflight

1

A. Pilot Qualifications

1. An applicant for an instrument rating must have at least how much and what type of flight time as pilot? (14 CFR 61.65)

A person who applies for an instrument–airplane rating must have logged the following:

a. 50 hours of cross-country flight time as PIC, of which 10 hours must have been in an airplane;

b. 40 hours of actual or simulated instrument time in the Part 61 areas of operation, of which 15 hours must have been received from an authorized instructor who holds an instrument airplane rating, and the instrument time includes:

   • 3 hours of instrument flight training from an authorized instructor in an airplane that is appropriate to the instrument–airplane rating within 2 calendar months before the date of the practical test;

   • Instrument flight training on cross country flight procedures, including one cross country flight in an airplane with an authorized instructor, that is performed under IFR, when a flight plan has been filed with an ATC facility, and that involves a flight of 250 NM along airways or ATC-directed routing, an instrument approach at each airport, and 3 different kinds of approaches with the use of navigation systems.

2. When is an instrument rating required? (14 CFR 61.3e, 91.157)

When operations are conducted:

a. Under instrument flight rules (IFR flight plan),

b. In weather conditions less than the minimum for VFR flight,

c. In Class A airspace,

d. Under Special VFR within Class B, Class C, Class D and Class E surface areas between sunset and sunrise.

e. When carrying passengers for hire on cross-country flights in excess of 50 nautical miles or at night.

3. What are the recency-of-experience requirements to be PIC of a flight under IFR? (14 CFR 61.57)

The recency-of-experience requirements are:

a. A flight review;

b. To carry passengers, 3 takeoffs and landings within the preceding 90 days in an aircraft of the same category, class and type, if a type rating is required (landings must be full stop at night or in a tailwheel).

c. Within the 6 calendar months preceding the month of the flight, performed and logged in actual weather conditions or under simulated conditions using a view-limiting device, at least the following tasks in an airplane:

   • Six instrument approaches.

   • Holding procedures and tasks.

   • Intercepting and tracking courses through the use of navigational electronic systems.

Note: 14 CFR §61.57(c) allows the use of an aircraft and/or a flight simulator, flight training device, or aviation training device for maintaining instrument experience, subject to certain limitations.

4. If a pilot allows his/her instrument currency to expire, what can be done to become current again? (14 CFR 61.57, 91.109)

A pilot is current for the first 6 months following his/her instrument checkride or proficiency check. If the pilot has not accomplished at least 6 approaches (including holding procedures, intercepting/tracking courses through the use of navigation systems) within this first 6 months, he/she is no longer legal to file and fly under IFR. To become legal again, the regulations allow a "grace period" (the second 6-month period), in which a pilot may get current by finding an "appropriately rated" safety pilot, and in simulated IFR conditions only, acquire the 6 approaches, etc. If the second 6-month period also passes without accomplishing the minimum, a pilot may reinstate his/her currency by accomplishing an instrument proficiency check given by an examiner, an authorized instructor, or an FAA-approved person to conduct instrument practical tests.

5. What are the required qualifications for a person to act as a "safety pilot"? (14 CFR 61.3, 61.23, and 91.109)

The safety pilot must:

a. Possess at least a private pilot certificate with category and class ratings appropriate to the aircraft being flown.

b. Possess an appropriate medical certificate (the safety pilot is acting as a required crewmember).

c. If the flight is to be conducted on an IFR flight plan, the person acting as PIC of the flight must hold an instrument rating and be instrument current.

6. What conditions are necessary for a pilot to log instrument time? (14 CFR 61.51)

A pilot may log as instrument flight time only that time during which he/she operates the aircraft solely by reference to instruments, under actual or simulated conditions.

7. When logging instrument time, what should be included in each logbook entry? (14 CFR 61.51)

Each entry must include the location and type of each instrument approach accomplished and the name of the safety pilot, if required.

8. What conditions must exist in order to log "actual" instrument flight time?

The FAA has never defined the term "actual" instrument time. 14 CFR Part 61 defines "instrument flight time" as that flight time when a person operates an aircraft solely by reference to instruments under actual or simulated instrument flight conditions. A reasonable guideline for determining when to log "actual instrument time" would be any flight time that is accumulated in IMC conditions with flight being conducted solely by reference to instruments. The definition of IMC is weather conditions below the VFR minimums specified for visual meteorological conditions. VFR minimums are found in 14 CFR §91.155.

9. What is the definition of the term "flight time"? (14 CFR Part 1)

Flight time means pilot time that commences when an aircraft moves under its own power for the purpose of flight and ends when the aircraft comes to rest after landing.

B. Preflight Action for Flight
(IFR or Flight Not in the Vicinity of Airport)

1. How can the use of the "PAVE" checklist during preflight help a pilot to assess and mitigate risk? (FAA-H-8083-9)

Use of the PAVE checklist provides pilots with a simple way to remember each category to examine for risk during flight planning. The pilot divides the risks of flight into four categories:

Pilot-In-Command—illness, medication, stress, alcohol, fatigue, emotion (I'M SAFE)

Aircraft—airworthiness, aircraft equipped for flight, proficiency in aircraft, performance capability

enVironment—weather hazards, type of terrain, airports/runways to be used, conditions

External pressures—meetings, people waiting at destination, desire to impress, desire to get there, etc.

2. What information must a pilot-in-command be familiar with before a flight? (14 CFR 91.103)

All available information including:

a. Weather reports and forecasts

b. Fuel requirements

c. Alternatives if the flight cannot be completed as planned

d. Known ATC delays

e. Runway lengths of intended use

f. Takeoff and landing distances

3. What are the fuel requirements for flight in IFR conditions? (14 CFR 91.167)

The aircraft must carry enough fuel to fly to the first airport of intended landing (including the approach), the alternate airport (if required), and thereafter, for 45 minutes at normal cruise speed. If an alternate airport is not required, enough fuel must be carried to fly to the destination airport and land with 45 minutes of fuel remaining.

4. Before conducting an IFR flight using GPS equipment for navigation, what basic preflight checks should be made? (FAA-H-8261-1)

Preflight preparations should include:

a. Verify that the GPS is properly installed and certified for the planned IFR operation.

b. Verify that the databases (navigation, terrain, obstacle, etc.) have not expired.

c. Review GPS and WAAS NOTAMs.

d. Review GPS RAIM availability for non-WAAS receivers.

e. Review operational status of ground-based NAVAIDs and related aircraft equipment (e.g., 30-day VOR check) appropriate to the route of flight, terminal operations, instrument approaches at the destination, and alternate airports at ETA.

5. Explain the function of RAIM. (FAA-H-8083-6)

Receiver autonomous integrity monitoring (RAIM) is the self-monitoring function performed by a TSO-129 certified GPS receiver to ensure that adequate GPS signals are being received at all times. The GPS alerts the pilot whenever the integrity monitoring determines that the GPS signals do not meet the criteria for safe navigation use.

6. When is a RAIM check required? (AIM 5-1-16)

TSO-C129 (non-WAAS) equipped aircraft—If TSO-C129 (non-WAAS) equipment is used to solely satisfy the RNAV and RNP requirement, GPS RAIM availability must be confirmed for the intended route of flight (route and time) using current GPS satellite information.

TSO-C145/C146 (WAAS) equipped aircraft—If TSO-C145/C146 (WAAS) equipment is used to satisfy the RNAV requirement, the pilot/operator need **not** perform the prediction if WAAS coverage is confirmed to be available along the entire route of flight. Outside the U.S. or in areas where WAAS coverage is not available, operators using TSO-C145/C146 receivers are required to check GPS RAIM availability.

Note: In the event of a predicted, continuous loss of RAIM of more than five (5) minutes for any part of the intended flight, the flight should be delayed, canceled, or re-routed where RAIM requirements can be met. Pilots should assess their capability to navigate (potentially to an alternate destination) in case of failure of GPS navigation.

7. What are several methods a pilot can use to satisfy the predictive RAIM requirement (RAIM check)? (AIM 5-1-16)

a. Operators may contact a FSS (not DUATS) to obtain non-precision approach RAIM. Briefers will provide RAIM information for a period of 1 hour before to 1 hour after the ETA, unless a specific time frame is requested by the pilot.

b. Use the FAA en route and terminal RAIM prediction website www.raimprediction.net.

c. Use a third-party interface, incorporating FAA/Volpe Center RAIM prediction data without altering performance values to predict RAIM outages for the aircraft's predicted flight path and times.

d. Use the receiver's installed RAIM prediction capability (for TSO-C129a/Class A1/B1/C1 equipment) to provide non-precision approach RAIM.

C. Preflight Action for Aircraft

1. Who is responsible for determining if an aircraft is in an airworthy condition? (14 CFR 91.7)

The pilot-in-command is responsible.

2. What aircraft instruments/equipment are required for IFR operations? (14 CFR 91.205)

Those required for VFR day and night flight plus:

G enerator or alternator of adequate capacity

R adios (nav. and comm. equipment suitable for the route to be flown)

A ltimeter (sensitive)

B all (slip/skid indicator of turn coordinator)

C lock (sweep second hand or digital presentation)

A ttitude indicator

R ate of turn (turn coordinator)

D irectional gyro

D ME or RNAV (for flight at FL240 and above if VOR equipment is required for the route)

3. What are the required tests and inspections of aircraft and equipment to be legal for IFR flight? (14 CFR 91.409, 91.403, 91.171, 91.411, 91.413, 91.207)

A Annual Inspection within the preceding 12 calendar months (14 CFR 91.409)

A Airworthiness Directives complied with as required (14 CFR 91.403)

V VOR check, if used for IFR, every 30 days (14 CFR 91.171)

1 100-hour inspection, if used for hire or flight instruction (14 CFR 91.409)

A Altimeter, altitude reporting equipment, and static pressure systems tested and inspected (for IFR ops), every 24 calendar months (14 CFR 91.411)

T Transponder tests and inspections, every 24 calendar months (14 CFR 91.413)

E Emergency locator transmitter, operation and battery condition inspected every 12 calendar months (14 CFR 91.207)

Continued

Note: Be capable of locating the last 100-hour/annual inspections in the aircraft and engine logbooks and be able to determine when the next inspections are due. Also, be capable of locating all required inspections for instruments/equipment necessary for legal VFR/IFR flight and determining that all ADs have been complied with.

4. May portable electronic devices be operated on board an aircraft? (14 CFR 91.21)

No person may operate nor may any PIC allow the operation of any portable electronic device:

a. On aircraft operated by an air carrier or commercial operator; or

b. On any other aircraft while it is operated under IFR.

Exceptions are: portable voice recorders, hearing aids, heart pace-makers, electric shavers or any other portable electronic device that the operator of the aircraft has determined will not cause interference with the navigation or communication system of the aircraft.

5. Are electronic chart systems (electronic flight bags) approved for use as a replacement for paper reference material (POH and supplements, charts, etc.) in the cockpit? (AC 91-78)

Yes; electronic flight bags (EFBs) can be used during all phases of flight operations in lieu of paper reference material when the information displayed is the functional equivalent of the paper reference material replaced and is current, up-to-date, and valid. It is recommended that a secondary or back-up source of aeronautical information necessary for the flight be available.

6. What documents must be on board an aircraft to make it legal for IFR flight? (14 CFR 91.9, 91.203)

A irworthiness Certificate
R egistration Certificate
R adio station license (if conducting international operations)
O wner's manual or operating limitations
W eight and balance data

7. **What additional aircraft documentation should be onboard an aircraft equipped with an IFR-approved GPS?** (FAA-H-8083-6)

   Most systems require an Airplane Flight Manual Supplement (AFMS) and Cockpit Reference Guide or Quick Reference Guide to be onboard as a limitation of use.

8. **How often are GPS databases required to be updated?** (FAA-H-8083-15)

   The navigation database is updated every 28 days. Obstacle databases may be updated every 56 days and terrain and airport map databases are updated as needed.

9. **Can a GPS with an expired database be used for navigation under IFR?** (AIM 1-1-18; AIM 5-1-16; AC 90-100)

   The navigation database contained in the GPS/FMS must be current if the system is to be used for IFR approaches. Some units allow enroute IFR operations with an expired database if the navigation waypoints are manually verified by referencing an official current source, such as a current enroute chart. To determine equipment approvals and limitations, refer to the AFM or AFM supplements.

   Note: The FAA-approved Airplane Flight Manual Supplement (required to be onboard the aircraft) is regulatory and specifies the requirements and operations permitted.

10. **Can a pilot perform the required database updates or must this action be accomplished by authorized maintenance personnel?** (14 CFR 43.3)

    Updates of databases of installed avionics may be performed by pilots provided they can be initiated from the flight deck, performed without disassembly of the avionics unit, and performed without the use of tools and/or special equipment.

11. When utilizing GPS for IFR navigation, are you required to have an alternate means of navigation appropriate for the route of flight? (AIM 1-1-18; FAA-H-8083-6)

Aircraft using GPS TSO-C129 or TSO-C196 (non-WAAS) navigation equipment under IFR must be equipped with an approved and operational alternate means of navigation appropriate to the flight. During preflight, ensure that this equipment is onboard and operational, and that all required checks have been performed (e.g., 30-day VOR check). Active monitoring of alternative navigation equipment is not required if the GPS receiver uses RAIM for integrity monitoring. Active monitoring of an alternate means of navigation is required when the RAIM capability of the GPS equipment is lost.

Note: Aircraft equipped with a WAAS receiver may use WAAS as a primary means of navigation. No additional equipment is required.

12. How can a pilot determine what type of operations a GPS receiver is approved for? (FAA-H-8083-6)

The pilot should reference the FAA-approved AFM and AFM supplements to determine the limitations and operating procedures for the particular GPS equipment installed.

13. Can a handheld GPS receiver be used for IFR operations? (AIM 1-1-18)

Visual flight rules (VFR) and hand-held GPS systems are not authorized for IFR navigation, instrument approaches, or as a principal instrument flight reference. During IFR operations they may be considered only as an aid to situational awareness.

D. IFR Flight Plan

1. When must a pilot file an IFR flight plan? (AIM 5-1-8)

Prior to departure from within or prior to entering controlled airspace, a pilot must submit a complete flight plan and receive clearance from ATC if weather conditions are below VFR minimums. The pilot should file the flight plan at least 30 minutes prior to the estimated time of departure to preclude a possible delay in receiving a departure clearance from ATC.

2. When will ATC delete from the system a departure flight plan that has not been activated? (AIM 5-1-13)

Most centers have this parameter set so as to delete these flight plans a minimum of 1 hour after the proposed departure time. To ensure that a flight plan remains active, pilots whose actual departure time will be delayed 1 hour or more beyond their filed departure time are requested to notify ATC of their revised departure time.

3. When can you cancel your IFR flight plan? (AIM 5-1-15)

An IFR flight plan may be canceled at any time the flight is operating in VFR conditions outside of Class A airspace. Pilots must be aware that other procedures may be applicable to a flight that cancels an IFR flight plan within an area where a special program, such as a designated TRSA, Class C airspace, or Class B airspace, has been established.

4. What is a composite flight plan? (AIM 5-1-7)

It is a flight plan that specifies VFR operation for one portion of a flight, and IFR for another.

5. After filing an IFR flight plan, can you depart VFR and pick up your IFR clearance in the air? (FAA-H-8261-1)

A VFR departure can be used as a tool that allows you to get off the ground without having to wait for a time slot in the IFR system; however, departing VFR with the intent of receiving an IFR clearance in the air can also present serious hazards worth considering. A VFR departure dramatically changes the takeoff responsibilities for you and for ATC:

a. Upon receiving clearance for a VFR departure, you are cleared to depart; however, you must maintain separation between yourself and other traffic.

b. You are also responsible for maintaining terrain and obstruction clearance as well as remaining in VFR weather conditions. You cannot fly in IMC without first receiving your IFR clearance.

c. Departing VFR relieves ATC of these duties, and basically requires them only to provide you with safety alerts as workload permits.

d. You must maintain VFR until you have obtained your IFR clearance and have ATC approval to proceed on course in accordance with your clearance. If you accept this clearance and are below the minimum IFR altitude for operations in the area, you accept responsibility for terrain/obstruction clearance until you reach that altitude.

6. The requested altitude on an FAA flight plan form (Block 7) represents which altitude for the route of flight—the initial, lowest, or highest? (AIM 5-1-8)

Enter only the initial requested altitude in this block. When more than one IFR altitude or flight level is desired along the route of flight, it is best to make a subsequent request direct to the controller.

7. What are the alternate airport requirements?
(14 CFR 91.169c)

1-2-3 Rule—If from 1 hour before to 1 hour after your planned ETA at the destination airport, the weather is forecast to be at least 2,000-foot ceilings and 3-mile visibilities, no alternate is required. If less than 2,000 and 3 miles, an alternate must be filed using the following criteria:

a. If an IAP is published for that airport, the alternate airport minimums specified in that procedure or, if none are specified, the following minimums—

  • Precision approach procedure: ceiling 600 feet and visibility 2 statute miles.

  • Nonprecision approaches: ceiling 800 feet and visibility 2 statute miles.

b. If no IAP has been published for that airport, the ceiling and visibility minimums are those allowing descent from the MEA, approach, and landing under basic VFR.

8. What is the definition of the term "ceiling"? (P/CG)

Ceiling is defined as the height above the Earth's surface of the lowest layer of clouds or obscuring phenomena reported as "broken," "overcast," or "obscuration," and not classified as "thin" or "partial."

9. What minimums are to be used on arrival at the alternate? (14 CFR 91.169c)

If an instrument approach procedure has been published for that airport, the minimums specified in that procedure are used.

10. What restrictions apply concerning filing an airport as an alternate when using TSO-C129 and TSO-C196 (non-WAAS) GPS equipment? (AIM 1-1-18)

TSO-C129 and TSO-C196 GPS-equipped users may file a flight plan for a GPS-based IAP at either the destination or the alternate airport, but not at both locations.

At the alternate airport, pilots may plan for applicable alternate airport weather minimums using:

a. LNAV or circling MDA.

b. LNAV/VNAV decision altitude (DA) if equipped with and using approved baro-VNAV equipment.

c. RNP 0.3 DA on an RNAV (RNP) IAP if specifically authorized with approved baro-VNAV equipment.

To take advantage of this option the pilot must:

a. Ensure the navigation system has fault detection and exclusion (FDE) capability.

b. Perform a preflight RAIM prediction at the airport where the RNAV (GPS) approach will be flown.

c. Have proper knowledge and any required training and/or approval to conduct a GPS-based IAP.

If the above conditions cannot be met, any required alternate airport must have an approved IAP other than GPS that is anticipated to be operational and available at the ETA, and which the aircraft is equipped to fly.

11. What instrument approach procedures may you flight plan to use as the planned approach at the required alternate when using TSO-C145/-C146 (WAAS) equipment? (AIM 1-1-19)

Pilots with TSO-C145/C146 WAAS receivers may flight plan to use any instrument approach procedure authorized for use with their WAAS avionics as the planned approach at a required alternate, with certain restrictions.

12. What restrictions apply to flight planning when using WAAS avionics at the alternate airport? (AIM 1-1-19)

When using WAAS avionics at an alternate airport, flight planning must be based on flying the RNAV (GPS) LNAV or circling minima line, or minima on a GPS approach procedure, or conventional approach procedure with "or GPS" in the title. 14 CFR Part 91 non-precision weather requirements must be used for planning. Upon arrival at an alternate, when the WAAS navigation system indicates that LNAV/VNAV or LPV service is available, then vertical guidance may be used to complete the approach using the displayed level of service.

E. Route Planning

1. What are preferred routes and where can they be found? (P/CG)

Preferred routes are those established between busier airports to increase system efficiency and capacity. Preferred routes are listed in the *Airport/Facility Directory.*

2. What are Enroute Low-Altitude Charts? (AIM 9-1-4)

Enroute low-altitude charts provide aeronautical information for navigation under IFR conditions below 18,000 feet MSL. These charts are revised every 56 days. All courses are magnetic and distances are nautical miles.

3. What are Enroute High-Altitude Charts? (AIM 9-1-4)

Enroute high-altitude charts are designed for navigation at or above 18,000 feet MSL. This four-color chart series includes the jet route structure; VHF NAVAIDs with frequency, identification, channel, geographic coordinates; selected airports; reporting points. Revised every 56 days.

4. What are "area charts"? (AIM 9-1-4)

Area charts show congested terminal areas such as Dallas/Ft. Worth or Atlanta at a large scale. They are included with subscriptions to any conterminous U.S. set Low (Full set, East or West sets). Revised every 56 days.

5. Where can information on possible navigational aid limitations be found? (FAA-H-8083-15)

NOTAMs as well as A/FDs will contain current limitations to NAVAIDs.

6. What other useful information can be found in the Airport/Facility Directory which might be helpful in route planning? (A/FD)

The A/FD contains additional information for each of the seven regions covered, such as:

a. Enroute Flight Advisory Services—locations and communications outlets.

b. ARTCC—locations and sector frequencies.

c. Aeronautical Chart Bulletins—recent changes after publication.

d. Preferred IFR routes—high and low altitude.

e. Special notices—flight service station, GADO, Weather Service office phone numbers.

f. VOR receiver checkpoints—locations and frequencies.

7. What are NOTAMs? (AIM 5-1-3)

Notices To Airmen (NOTAM)—Time critical aeronautical information, which is of either a temporary nature or not known sufficiently in advance to permit publication on aeronautical charts or in other operational publications, receives immediate dissemination via the National NOTAM System. It is aeronautical information that could affect a pilot's decision to make a flight. It includes such information as airport or primary runway closures, changes in the status of navigational aids, ILS's, radar service availability, and other information essential to planned en route, terminal, or landing operations.

8. **Explain the following types of NOTAMs: (D) NOTAMS, FDC NOTAMs, Pointer NOTAMs, Military NOTAMs, and SAA NOTAMs.** (AIM 5-1-3)

   a. *(D) NOTAMs*—Information that requires wide dissemination via telecommunication, regarding enroute navigational aids, civil public-use airports listed in the A/FD, facilities, services, and procedures.

   b. *FDC NOTAMs*—Flight information that is regulatory in nature including, but not limited to, changes to IFR charts, procedures, and airspace usage.

   c. *POINTER NOTAMs*—issued by a flight service station to highlight or point out another NOTAM; for example, an FDC NOTAM. These NOTAMs assist users in cross-referencing important information that may not be found under an airport or NAVAID identifier.

   d. *MILITARY NOTAMs*—these pertain to U.S. Air Force, Army, Marine, and Navy navigational aids/airports that are part of the NAS.

   e. *SAA NOTAMs*—issued when Special Activity Airspace will be active outside the published schedule times and when required; SAA includes special use airspace (restricted area, military operations area [MOA], warning area, and alert area airspace), instrument and visual military training routes, aerial refueling tracks and anchors.

9. **All (D) NOTAMs will have keywords contained within the first part of the text. What are several examples of these keywords?** (AIM 5-1-3)

   RWY, TWY, APRON, AD, OBST, NAV, COM, SVC,AIRSPACE, ODP, SID, STAR, CHART, DATA, IAP, VFP, ROUTE, SPECIAL, SECURITY, (U) or (O).

10. Where can NOTAM information be obtained? (AIM 5-1-3)

a. AFSS/FSS

b. DUATS vendors

c. NTAP printed NOTAMs. Published every 28 days; once published, these NOTAMS are not provided during pilot weather briefings unless specifically requested by the pilot. The NTAP is available online at the FAA's website: www.faa.gov/air_traffic/publications/notices/

d. NOTAMs are available at the FAA website: https://pilotweb.nas.faa.gov/PilotWeb/

11. How can a pilot obtain the latest GPS NOTAMS? (AIM 1-1-18)

A pilot can specifically request GPS aeronautical information from a FSS during preflight briefings.

12. What does the term "UNRELIABLE" indicate when used in conjunction with GPS and WAAS NOTAMs? (AIM 1-1-19)

The term UNRELIABLE is an advisory to pilots indicating the expected level of WAAS service (LNAV/VNAV, LPV) may not be available. WAAS UNRELIABLE NOTAMs are predictive in nature and published for flight planning purposes. Upon commencing an approach at locations NOTAMed WAAS UNRELIABLE and where the WAAS avionics indicate LNAV/VNAV or LPV service is available, vertical guidance may be used to complete the approach using the displayed level of service. If an outage occurs during the approach, reversion to LNAV minima may be required.

13. When flight planning an RNAV route, where should your route begin and end? (AIM 5-1-8)

Plan the random route portion of the flight plan to begin and end over appropriate arrival and departure transition fixes or appropriate navigation aids for the altitude stratum within which the flight will be conducted. The use of normal preferred departure and arrival routes (DP/STAR), where established, is recommended.

F. Flight Instruments

Pitot/Static System

1. What instruments operate from the pitot/static system? (FAA-H-8083-15)

The pitot/static system operates the altimeter, vertical-speed indicator, and airspeed indicator. All three instruments receive static air pressure for operation with only the ASI receiving both pitot and static pressure.

2. How does an altimeter work? (FAA-H-8083-15)

In an altimeter, aneroid wafers expand and contract as atmospheric pressure changes, and through a shaft and gear linkage, rotate pointers on the dial of the instrument.

3. What type of errors is the altimeter subject to? (FAA-H-8083-15)

a. Mechanical errors—Differences between ambient temperature and/or pressure can cause an erroneous indication on the altimeter.

b. Inherent errors—Non-standard temperature and pressure.

Warmer than standard air—The air is less dense and the pressure levels are farther apart. The pressure level for a given altitude is higher than it would be in air at standard temperature, and the aircraft is higher than it would be if the air were cooler. True altitude is higher than indicated altitude whenever the temperature is warmer than International Standard Atmosphere (ISA).

Colder than standard air—The air is denser and the pressure levels are closer together. The pressure level for a given altitude is lower than it would be in air at standard temperature, and the aircraft is lower than it would be if the air were warmer. True altitude is lower than indicated altitude whenever the temperature is colder than ISA.

Continued

Extreme cold altimeter errors—A correctly calibrated pressure altimeter indicates true altitude above mean sea level (MSL) when operating within ISA parameters of pressure and temperature. When operating in extreme cold temperatures (i.e., +10°C to -50°C), pilots may wish to compensate for the reduction in terrain clearance by adding a cold temperature correction.

High pressure to low pressure—If an aircraft is flown from an area of high pressure to an area of lower pressure without adjusting the altimeter, the true altitude of the aircraft will be lower than indicated altitude.

Low pressure to high pressure—If an aircraft is flown from an area of low pressure to an area of higher pressure without adjusting the altimeter, the true altitude of the aircraft will be higher than indicated altitude.

Remember: High to Low or Hot to Cold—look out below!

4. For IFR flight, what is the maximum allowable error for an altimeter? (FAA-H-8083-15)

If the altimeter is off field elevation by more than 75 feet, with the correct pressure set in the Kollsman window, it is considered to be unreliable.

5. Define and state how to determine the following altitudes:

Indicated altitude
True altitude
Absolute altitude
Pressure altitude
Density altitude

(FAA-H-8083-25)

Indicated altitude—read directly from the altimeter when set to the current altimeter setting.

True altitude—the vertical distance of the aircraft above sea level (MSL). Airport, terrain, and obstacle elevations on aeronautical charts are true altitudes.

Absolute altitude—the vertical distance of an aircraft above the terrain, or above ground level (AGL). It may be read on a radio/radar altimeter.

Pressure altitude—indicated altitude with altimeter set to 29.92 in. Hg. Pressure altitude is used to compute density altitude, true altitude, true airspeed (TAS), and other performance data.

Density altitude—pressure altitude corrected for variations from standard temperature.

6. How does the airspeed indicator operate? (FAA-H-8083-15)

The airspeed indicator measures the difference between ram pressure from the pitot head and atmospheric pressure from the static source.

7. What are the limitations the airspeed indicator is subject to? (FAA H 8083-15)

It must have proper flow of air in the pitot/static system.

8. What are the errors that the airspeed indicator is subject to?

Position error—caused by the static ports sensing erroneous static pressure; slipstream flow causes disturbances at the static port preventing actual atmospheric pressure measurement. It varies with airspeed, altitude, configuration and may be a plus or minus value.

Density error—changes in altitude and temperature are not compensated for by the instrument.

Compressibility error—caused by the packing of air into the pitot tube at high airspeeds, resulting in higher than normal indications. It usually occurs above 180 KIAS.

9. **What are the different types of aircraft speeds?**
   (FAA-H-8083-15)

   Indicated Airspeed (IAS)—IAS is shown on the dial of the instrument, uncorrected for instrument or system errors.

   Calibrated Airspeed (CAS)—CAS is the speed at which the aircraft is moving through the air, which is found by correcting IAS for instrument and position errors. The POH/AFM has a chart or graph to correct IAS for these errors and provide the correct CAS for the various flap and landing gear configurations.

   Equivalent Airspeed (EAS)—EAS is CAS corrected for compression of the air inside the pitot tube. EAS is the same as CAS in standard atmosphere at sea level. As the airspeed and pressure altitude increase, the CAS becomes higher than it should be, and a correction for compression must be subtracted from the CAS.

   True Airspeed (TAS)—TAS is CAS corrected for nonstandard pressure and temperature. TAS and CAS are the same in standard atmosphere at sea level. Under nonstandard conditions, TAS is found by applying a correction for pressure altitude and temperature to the CAS.

10. **What airspeeds are indicated by the various color codes found on the dial of an airspeed indicator?**
    (FAA-H-8083-25)

White arc	flap operating range
Lower limit of white arc (V_{S0})	stall speed or minimum steady flight speed in landing configuration (gear and flaps down)
Upper limit of the white arc (V_{FE})	maximum speed with the flaps extended
Green arc	normal operating range
Lower limit of green arc (V_{S1})	stall speed or minimum steady flight speed obtained in a specified or clean configuration

Upper limit of green arc (V_{NO})	maximum structural cruising speed. Do not exceed this speed except in smooth air.
Yellow arc	caution range; fly within this range only in smooth air, and then, only with caution.
Red line (V_{NE})	never exceed speed; operating above this speed is prohibited; may result in damage or structural failure.

11. How does the vertical-speed indicator work?
(FAA-H-8083-15)

The VSI is a rate-of-pressure-change instrument that gives an indication of any deviation from a constant pressure level. Inside the VSI instrument case is an aneroid. Both the inside of the aneroid and the inside of the instrument case are vented to the static system. The case is vented through a calibrated orifice that causes the pressure inside the case to change more slowly than the pressure inside the aneroid. Changing pressures inside the case and the aneroid compress and expand the aneroid, moving the pointer upward or downward indicating a climb, a descent, or level flight.

12. What are the limitations of the vertical-speed indicator?
(FAA-H-8083-15)

It is not accurate until the aircraft is stabilized. Sudden or abrupt changes in the aircraft attitude will cause erroneous instrument readings as airflow fluctuates over the static port. These changes are not reflected immediately by the VSI due to the calibrated leak.

13. What instruments are affected when the pitot tube, ram air inlet, and drain hole freeze? (FAA-H-8083-25)

Only the airspeed indicator will be affected. It acts like an altimeter—it will read higher as the aircraft climbs and lower as the aircraft descends. It reads lower than actual speed in level flight.

14. What instruments are affected when the static port freezes? (FAA-H-8083-25)

Airspeed indicator—Accurate at the altitude frozen as long as static pressure in the indicator and the system equals outside pressure. If the aircraft descends, the airspeed indicator would read high (outside static pressure would be greater than that trapped). If the aircraft climbs, the airspeed indicator would read low.

Altimeter—Indicates the altitude at which the system is blocked.

Vertical speed—Will indicate level flight.

15. If the air temperature is +6°C at an airport elevation of 1,200 feet and a standard (average) temperature lapse rate exists, what will be the approximate freezing level?

4,200 MSL; 6° at the surface divided by the average temperature lapse rate of 2°C results in a 3,000-foot freezing level, converted to sea level by adding the 1,200-foot airport elevation.

16. What corrective action is needed if the pitot tube freezes? If the static port freezes? (FAA-H-8083-15)

For pitot tube—Turn pitot heat on.

For static system—Use alternate air if available or break the face of a static instrument (either the VSI or A/S indicator).

17. What indications should you expect while using alternate air? (FAA-H-8083-25)

In many unpressurized aircraft equipped with a pitot-static tube, an alternate source of static pressure is provided for emergency use. If the alternate source is vented inside the airplane where static pressure is usually lower than outside, selection of the alternate static source may result in the following indications:

Altimeter.. will indicate higher than the actual altitude

Airspeed.. will indicate greater than the actual airspeed

Vertical speed .... will indicate a climb while in level flight

Note: Always consult the AFM/POH to determine the amount of error.

Gyroscopic System

1. What instruments contain gyroscopes? (FAA-H-8083-15)

Attitude indicator, heading indicator and turn coordinator/indicator.

2. Name several types of power sources commonly used to power the gyroscopic instruments in an aircraft. (FAA-H-8083-15)

Various power sources used are: electrical, pneumatic, venturi tube, wet-type vacuum pump, and dry-air pump systems. Aircraft and instrument manufacturers have designed redundancy into the flight instruments so that any single failure will not deprive the pilot of his/her ability to safely conclude the flight. Gyroscopic instruments are crucial for instrument flight; therefore, they are powered by separate electrical or pneumatic sources. Typically, the heading indicator and attitude indicator will be vacuum-driven and the turn coordinator electrically-driven.

Note: It is extremely important that pilots consult the POH/AFM to determine the power source of all instruments to know what action to take in the event of an instrument failure.

3. How does the vacuum system operate? (FAA-H-8083-25)

The vacuum or pressure system spins the gyro by drawing a stream of air against the rotor vanes to spin the rotor at high speeds, essentially the same as a water wheel or turbine operates. The amount of vacuum or pressure required for instrument operation varies by manufacturer and is usually between 4.5 to 5.5 in. Hg. One source of vacuum for the gyros installed in light aircraft is the vane-type engine-driven pump, mounted on the accessory case of the engine.

4. What are two important characteristics of gyroscopes?
(FAA-H-8083-15)

Rigidity—the characteristic of a gyro that prevents its axis of rotation tilting as the Earth rotates; attitude and heading instruments operate on this principle.

Precession—the characteristic of a gyro that causes an applied force to be felt, not at the point of application, but 90 degrees from that point in the direction of rotation. Rate instruments such as the turn coordinator use this principle.

5. How does the turn coordinator operate? (FAA-H-8083-15)

The turn part of the instrument uses precession to indicate direction and approximate rate of turn. A gyro reacts by trying to move in reaction to the force applied, thus moving the miniature aircraft in proportion to the rate of turn. The inclinometer in the instrument is a black glass ball sealed inside a curved glass tube that is partially filled with a liquid. The ball measures the relative strength of the force of gravity and the force of inertia caused by a turn.

6. What information does the turn coordinator provide?
(FAA-H-8083-15)

The miniature aircraft in the turn coordinator displays the rate of turn, rate of roll and direction of turn. The ball in the tube indicates the quality of turn (slip or skid).

Slip—ball on the inside of turn; not enough rate of turn for the amount of bank.

Skid—ball to the outside of turn; too much rate of turn for the amount of bank.

7. What is the source of power for the turn coordinator?
(FAA-H-8083-15)

Turn coordinator gyros can be driven by either air or electricity; some are dual-powered. Typically the turn coordinator is electrically powered, but always refer to the AFM for specifics.

8. How does the heading indicator work? (FAA-H-8083-25)

The operation of the heading indicator works on the principle of rigidity in space. The rotor turns in a vertical plane, and fixed to the rotor is a compass card. Since the rotor remains rigid in space, the points on the card hold the same position in space relative to the vertical plane. As the instrument case and the airplane revolve around the vertical axis, the card provides clear and accurate heading information.

9. What are the limitations of the heading indicator? (FAA-H-8083-25)

They vary with the particular design and make of instrument: on some heading indicators in light airplanes, the limits are approximately 55 degrees of pitch and 55 degrees of bank. When either of these attitude limits are exceeded, the instrument "tumbles" or "spills" and no longer gives the correct indication until it is reset with the caging knob. Many modern instruments used are designed in such a manner that they will not tumble.

10. What type of error is the heading indicator subject to? (FAA-H-8083-25)

Because of precession (caused by friction), the heading indicator will creep or drift from the heading it is set to. The amount of drift depends largely upon the condition of the instrument (worn and dirty bearings and/or improperly lubricated bearings). Additionally, the gyro is oriented in space and the earth rotates in space at a rate of 15 degrees in 1 hour; therefore, discounting precession caused by friction, the heading indicator may indicate as much as 15 degrees of error per every hour of operation.

11. How does the attitude indicator work? (FAA-H-8083-25)

The gyro in the attitude indicator is mounted on a horizontal plane and depends upon rigidity in space for its operation. The horizon bar represents the true horizon and is fixed to the gyro; it remains in a horizontal plane as the airplane is pitched or banked about its lateral or longitudinal axis, indicating the attitude of the airplane relative to the true horizon.

12. What are the limitations of an attitude indicator? (FAA-H-8083-25)

Limits depend upon the make and model of the instrument; bank limits are usually from 100° to 110°, and pitch limits are usually from 60° to 70°. If either limit is exceeded, the instrument will tumble or spill and will give incorrect indications until restabilized. Some modern attitude indicators are designed so they will not tumble.

13. Is the attitude indicator subject to errors? (FAA-H-8083-15)

Attitude indicators are free from most errors, but depending upon the speed with which the erection system functions, there may be a slight nose-up indication during a rapid acceleration and a nose-down indication during a rapid deceleration. There is also a possibility of a small bank angle and pitch error after a 180° turn. On rollout from a 180° turn, the AI will indicate a slight climb and turn in the opposite direction of rollout. These inherent errors are small and correct themselves within a minute or so after returning to straight-and-level flight.

Magnetic Compass

1. How does the magnetic compass work? (FAA-H-8083-15)

Magnets mounted on the compass card align themselves parallel to the Earth's lines of magnetic force.

2. What limitations does the magnetic compass have? (FAA-H-8083-15)

The jewel-and-pivot type mounting gives the float freedom to rotate and tilt up to approximately 18° angle of bank. At steeper bank angles, the compass indications are erratic and unpredictable.

3. What are the various compass errors? (FAA-H-8083-15)

Oscillation error—Erratic movement of the compass card caused by turbulence or rough control technique.

Deviation error—Due to electrical and magnetic disturbances in the aircraft.

Variation error—Angular difference between true and magnetic north; reference isogonic lines of variation.

Dip errors:

a. *Acceleration error*—On east or west headings, while accelerating, the magnetic compass shows a turn to the north, and when decelerating, it shows a turn to the south.

   Remember: ANDS—Accelerate North, Decelerate South

b. *Northerly turning error*—When turning in a northerly direction, the compass float assembly leads rather than lags resulting in a false northerly turn indication. Because of this lead of the compass card, or float assembly, a northerly turn should be stopped prior to arrival at the desired heading.

c. *Southerly turning error*—When turning in a southerly direction, the compass float assembly lags rather than leads resulting in a false southerly turn indication. The compass card, or float assembly, should be allowed to pass the desired heading prior to stopping the turn.

   Remember: UNOS—Undershoot North, Overshoot South

Electronic Flight Instrument Displays

1. Describe the function of the following avionics equipment acronyms: PFD, MFD, AHRS, ADC, FMS, FD, TAWS, TIS. (FAA-H-8083-6)

PFD—primary flight display. A PFD provides increased situational awareness to the pilot by replacing the traditional six instruments used for instrument flight with an easy-to-scan display that provides the horizon, airspeed, altitude, vertical speed, trend, trim, and rate of turn, among other key indications.

MFD—multi-function display. A cockpit display capable of presenting information such as navigation data, moving maps, aircraft systems information (engine monitoring), or should the need arise, PFD information.

AHRS—attitude and heading reference system. An integrated flight system composed of three-axis sensors that provide heading, attitude, and yaw information for an aircraft. GPS, solid state

Continued

magnetometers, solid state accelerometers, and digital air data signals are all combined in an AHRS to compute and output highly reliable information to the cockpit primary flight display.

ADC—air data computer. An aircraft computer that receives and processes ram air, static air, and temperature information from sensors, and provides information such as altitude, indicated airspeed, vertical speed, and wind direction and velocity to other cockpit systems (PFD, AHRS, transponder).

FMS—flight management system. A computer system containing a database to allow programming of routes, approaches, and departures that can supply navigation data to the flight director/ autopilot from various sources, and can calculate flight data such as fuel consumption, time remaining, possible range, and other values.

FD—flight director. An electronic flight calculator that analyzes the navigation selections, signals, and aircraft parameters. It presents steering instructions on the flight display as command bars or crossbars for the pilot to position the nose of the aircraft over or follow.

TAWS—terrain awareness and warning system. Uses the aircraft's GPS navigation signal and altimetry systems to compare the position and trajectory of the aircraft against a more detailed terrain and obstacle database. This database attempts to detail every obstruction that could pose a threat to an aircraft in flight.

TIS—Traffic Information Service is a ground-based advanced avionics traffic display system which receives transmissions on locations of nearby aircraft from radar-equipped air traffic control facilities and provides alerts and warnings to the pilot.

2. What is the function of a magnetometer? (FAA-H-8083-6)

A magnetometer is a device that measures the strength of the earth's magnetic field to determine aircraft heading. It provides this information digitally to the AHRS, which relays it to the PFD.

3. **Does an aircraft have to remain stationary during AHRS system initialization?** (FAA-H-8083-6)

Some AHRSs must be initialized on the ground prior to departure. The initialization procedure allows the system to establish a reference attitude used as a benchmark for all future attitude changes. Other systems are capable of initialization while taxiing as well as in-flight.

4. **If a failure of one of the displays (PFD or MFD) occurs in an aircraft with an electronic flight display, what will happen to the remaining operative display?** (FAA-H-8083-6)

In the event of a display failure, some systems offer a "reversion" capability to display the primary flight instruments and engine instruments on the remaining operative display.

5. **When a display failure occurs, what other system components will be affected?** (AFM/POH)

In some systems, failure of a display will also result in partial loss of navigation, communication, and GPS capability. Reference your specific AFM/POH.

6. **What display information will be affected when an ADC failure occurs?** (FAA-H 8083-6)

Inoperative airspeed, altitude, and vertical speed indicators (red Xs) on the PFD indicate the failure of the air data computer.

7. **What display information will be lost when an AHRS failure occurs?** (FAA-H-8083-6)

An inoperative attitude indicator (red X) on a PFD indicates failure of the AHRS.

8. **How will loss of a magnetometer affect the AHRS operation?** (FAA-H-8083-6)

Heading information will be lost.

G. Fundamentals of Weather

1. **At what rate does atmospheric pressure decrease with an increase in altitude?** (AC 00-6)

   Atmospheric pressure decreases approximately 1" Hg per 1,000 feet.

2. **What are the standard temperature and pressure values for sea level?** (AC 00-6)

   15°C and 29.92" Hg are standard at sea level.

3. **State the general characteristics in regard to the flow of air around high and low pressure systems in the northern hemisphere.** (AC 00-6)

   Low pressure—Air flows inward, upward, and counterclockwise.

   High pressure—Air flows outward, downward, and clockwise.

4. **What causes the winds aloft to flow parallel to the isobars?** (AC 00-6)

   The Coriolis force causes winds aloft to flow parallel to the isobars.

5. **Why do surface winds generally flow across the isobars at an angle?** (AC 00-6)

   Surface friction causes winds to flow across isobars at an angle.

6. **When temperature and dew point are close together (within 5°), what type of weather is likely?** (AC 00-6)

   Visible moisture is likely, in the form of clouds, dew or fog.

7. **What factor primarily determines the type and vertical extent of clouds?** (AC 00-6)

   The stability of the atmosphere determines type and vertical extent of clouds.

8. **What is the difference between a stable and an unstable atmosphere?** (AC 00-6)

   A stable atmosphere resists any upward or downward displacement. An unstable atmosphere allows an upward or downward disturbance to grow into a vertical or convective current.

9. **How do you determine the stability of the atmosphere?** (AC 00-6)

   When temperature decreases uniformly and rapidly as you climb (approaching 3°C per 1,000 feet), you have an indication of unstable air. If the temperature remains unchanged or decreases only slightly with altitude, the air tends to be stable. When air near the surface is warm and moist, suspect instability.

10. **List the effects of stable and unstable air on clouds, turbulence, precipitation and visibility.** (AC 00-6)

	Stable	Unstable
Clouds	Stratiform	Cumuliform
Turbulence	Smooth	Rough
Precipitation	Steady	Showery
Visibility	Fair to Poor	Good

11. **What are the main types of icing an aircraft may encounter?** (AC 00-6)

   Structural, induction system, and instrument icing.

12. **Name the three types of structural ice that may occur in flight.** (AC 00-6)

Clear ice—forms after initial impact when the remaining liquid portion of the drop flows out over the aircraft surface, gradually freezing as a smooth sheet of solid ice; air temperature range conducive for this type of ice to form is 0°C to -10°C.

Rime ice—forms when drops are small, such as those in stratified clouds or light drizzle. The liquid portion remaining after initial impact freezes rapidly before the drop has time to spread out over the aircraft surface; air temperature range most conducive for this type of ice to form is -15°C to -20°C.

Mixed ice—forms when drops vary in size or when liquid drops are intermingled with snow or ice particles. The ice particles become embedded in clear ice, building a very rough accumulation; air temperature range most conducive for this type of ice to form is -10°C to -15°C.

13. **What is necessary for structural icing to occur?** (AC 00-6)

The aircraft must be flying through visible water such as rain or cloud droplets; temperature must be at the point where moisture strikes the aircraft at 0°C or colder.

14. **What are the intensity categories of aircraft structural icing?** (AC 00-45)

   a. *Trace*—ice becomes perceptible; rate of accumulation slightly greater than sublimation; deicing/anti-icing equipment is not used unless encountered for extended period of time (over 1 hour).

   b. *Light*—rate of accumulation may create a problem if flight is prolonged in this environment (over 1 hour). Occasional use of deicing/anti-icing equipment removes or prevents accumulation.

   c. *Moderate*—the rate of accumulation is such that even short encounters become potentially hazardous; use of deicing/anti-icing equipment or diversion is necessary.

   d. *Severe*—rate of accumulation is such that deicing/anti-icing equipment fails to reduce or control the hazard; immediate diversion is necessary.

15. **During preflight planning, what type of meteorological information should you be aware of with respect to icing?** (AC 91-74)

   a. *Location of fronts*—the front's location, type, speed, and direction of movement.

   b. *Cloud layers*—the location of cloud bases and tops; this is valuable when determining if you will be able to climb above icing layers or descend beneath those layers into warmer air.

   c. *Freezing level(s)*—important when determining how to avoid icing and how to exit icing conditions if accidentally encountered.

   d. *Air temperature and pressure*—icing tends to be found in low-pressure areas and at temperatures at or around freezing.

   e. *Precipitation*—knowing the location and type of precipitation forecast will assist in avoiding areas conducive to severe icing.

16. **What is the definition of the term "freezing level" and how can you determine where that level is?** (AC 00-6)

   The freezing level is the lowest altitude in the atmosphere over a given location at which the air temperature reaches 0°C. It is possible to have multiple freezing layers when a temperature inversion occurs above the defined freezing level. Potential sources of icing information for determining its location are: area forecasts, PIREPS, AIRMETs, SIGMETs, convective SIGMETS, low-level significant weather charts, surface analysis (for frontal location and freezing precipitation) and winds and temperatures aloft (for air temperature at altitude). Pilots can use graphical data including freezing level graphics, the current icing product (CIP), and forecast icing product (FIP). These products are available at the NWS Aviation Digital Data Service (ADDS) website: www.aviationweather.gov/adds/icing/

17. What are the factors necessary for a thunderstorm to form and what are the three stages of thunderstorm development? (AC 00-6)

For a thunderstorm to form, the air must have sufficient water vapor, an unstable lapse rate, and an initial upward boost (lifting) to start the storm process in motion. During its lifecycle, a thunderstorm cell progresses through three stages:

a. *Cumulus*—characterized by a strong updraft.

b. *Mature*—precipitation beginning to fall from the cloud base signals that a downdraft has developed and a cell has entered the mature stage.

c. *Dissipating*—downdrafts characterize the dissipating stage and the storm dies rapidly.

18. What are "squall line" thunderstorms? (AC 00-6)

A squall line is a non-frontal, narrow band of active thunderstorms. Often it develops ahead of a cold front in moist, unstable air, but it may also develop in unstable air far removed from any front. The line may be too long to easily detour and too wide and severe to penetrate. It often contains severe steady-state thunderstorms and presents the single most intense weather hazard to aircraft. It usually forms rapidly, reaching a maximum intensity during the late afternoon and the first few hours of darkness.

19. State two basic ways that fog may form. (AC 00-6)

Fog forms:

a. By cooling air to the dew point

b. By adding moisture to the air

20. Name several types of fog. (AC 00-6)

a. Radiation fog

b. Advection fog

c. Upslope fog

d. Precipitation-induced fog

e. Ice fog

21. What causes radiation fog to form? (AC 00-6)

Conditions favorable for radiation fog are a clear sky, little or no wind, and small temperature-dew point spread (high relative humidity). The fog forms almost exclusively at night or near daybreak.

22. What is advection fog, and where is it most likely to form? (AC 00-6)

Advection fog forms when moist air moves over colder ground or water. It is most common along coastal areas but often develops deep in continental areas. Unlike radiation fog, it may occur with winds, cloudy skies, over a wide geographic area, and at any time of the day or night. It deepens as wind speed increases up to about 15 knots; wind much stronger than 15 knots lifts the fog into a layer of low stratus or stratocumulus.

23. Define upslope fog. (AC 00-6)

Upslope fog forms as a result of moist, stable air being cooled adiabatically as it moves up sloping terrain. Once the upslope wind ceases, the fog dissipates. Unlike radiation fog, it can form under cloudy skies. It is common along the eastern slopes of the Rockies and somewhat less frequent east of the Appalachians; can often be quite dense and extend to high altitudes.

24. Define ice fog. (AC 00-6)

Ice fog occurs in cold weather when the temperature is much below freezing and water vapor sublimates directly as ice crystals. Conditions favorable for its formation are the same as for radiation fog except for cold temperature, usually -25°F or colder. It occurs mostly in the Arctic regions, but is not unknown in middle latitudes during the cold season. Ice fog can be quite blinding to someone flying into the sun.

25. What is precipitation-induced fog? (AC 00-6)

When relatively warm rain or drizzle falls through cool air, evaporation from the precipitation saturates the cool air and forms fog. Precipitation-induced fog can become quite dense and continue for an extended period of time. This fog may extend over large areas, completely suspending air operations. It is most commonly associated with warm fronts, but can occur with slow-moving cold fronts and with stationary fronts.

26. Other than fog, what are several other examples of IFR weather producers? (AC 00-6)

Other examples of common IFR producers are low clouds (stratus), haze, smoke, blowing obstructions to vision, and precipitation. Fog and low stratus restrict navigation by visual reference more often than all other weather phenomena.

H. Obtaining Weather Information

1. What is the primary means of obtaining a weather briefing? (AIM 7-1-2)

The primary source of preflight weather briefings is an individual briefing obtained from a briefer at the AFSS/FSS.

2. What are some examples of other sources of weather information? (AIM 7-1-2)

a. Telephone Information Briefing Service (TIBS) (FSS)

b. Weather and aeronautical information available from numerous private industry sources

c. The Direct User Access Terminal System (DUATS)

d. Inflight weather information is available from a FSS on a common frequency of 122.2 MHz.

3. What pertinent information should a weather briefing Include? (AIM 7-1-4)

a. Adverse conditions

b. VFR flight not recommended

c. Synopsis

d. Current conditions

e. Enroute forecast

f. Destination forecast

g. Winds aloft

h. Notices to Airmen (NOTAMs)

i. ATC delay

In addition, pilots may obtain the following from FSS briefers upon request: information on special use airspace (SUA) and SUA-related airspace, including alert areas, MOAs, MTRs (IFR, VFR, VR, and SR training routes), warning areas, and ATC assigned airspace (ATCAA); a review of the printed NOTAM publication; approximate density altitude data; information on air traffic services and rules; customs/immigration procedures; ADIZ rules; search and rescue; GPS RAIM availability for 1 hour before to 1 hour after ETA or a time specified by the pilot; and other assistance as required

4. What is "EFAS"? (AIM 7-1-5)

Enroute Flight Advisory Service (EFAS) is a service specifically designed to provide enroute aircraft with timely and meaningful weather advisories pertinent to the type of flight intended, route of flight, and altitude. EFAS is also a central collection and distribution point for pilot-reported weather information (PIREPs). EFAS provides communications capabilities for aircraft flying at 5,000 feet above ground level to 17,500 feet MSL on a common frequency of 122.0 MHz. It is also known as "Flight Watch." Discrete EFAS frequencies have been established to ensure communications coverage from 18,000 through 45,000 feet MSL, serving in each specific ARTCC area. These discrete frequencies may be used below 18,000 feet when coverage permits reliable communication.

5. What is "HIWAS"? (AIM 7-1-10)

Hazardous Inflight Weather Advisory Service (HIWAS) is an automated continuous broadcast of inflight weather advisories including summarized Aviation Weather Warnings, SIGMETs, Convective SIGMETs, Center Weather Advisories, AIRMETs, and urgent PIREPs. HIWAS is an additional source of hazardous weather information which makes this data available on a continuous basis.

6. What is Flight Information Service (FIS) and how does it work? (AIM 7-1-11)

Aviation weather and other operational information may be displayed in the cockpit through the use of FIS. FIS systems are of two basic types: Broadcast only systems (called FIS-B) and two-way request/reply systems. Broadcast system components include a ground- or space-based transmitter, an aircraft receiver, and a portable or installed cockpit display device. Two-way systems utilize transmitter/receivers at both the ground or space-based site and the aircraft. FIS is available through an FAA-operated service using a broadcast data link on the (ADS-B) UAT network as well as from numerous private providers. FIS is not intended to replace traditional pilot and controller, flight service specialist, or aircraft dispatcher pre-flight briefings or inflight voice communications.

I. Aviation Weather Reports and Observations

1. What is a METAR? (AC 00-45)

The aviation routine weather report (METAR) is the weather observer's interpretation of the weather conditions at a given site and time. There are two types of METAR reports: a routine METAR report that is transmitted every hour and an aviation selected special weather report (SPECI). This is a special report that can be given at any time to update the METAR for rapidly changing weather conditions, aircraft mishaps, or other critical information.

2. Describe the basic elements of a METAR. (AC 00-45)

A METAR report contains the following elements in the order presented:

a. *Type of report*—the METAR (routine), and SPECI (special observation).

b. *Station identifier*— (ICAO) four-letter station identifier; in the conterminous United States, the three letter identifier is prefixed with K.

c. *Date and time of report*—six-digit date/time group appended with Z to denote Coordinated Universal Time (UTC). The first two digits are the date followed with two digits for hour and two digits for minutes.

d. *Modifier (as required)*—if used AUTO identifies a METAR/ SPECI report as an automated weather report with no human intervention.

e. *Wind*—five-digit group (six digits if speed is over 99 knots); first three digits, direction of the wind from in tens of degrees referenced to true north. Directions less than 100 degrees are preceded with a zero; next two digits are average speed in knots, measured or estimated, or if over 99 knots, the next three digits.

f. *Visibility*—prevailing visibility in statute miles followed by a space, fractions of statute miles, as needed, and the letters SM.

g. *Runway visual range (RVR) (as required)*—follows the visibility element.

h. *Weather phenomena*—broken into two categories: qualifiers and weather phenomena.

i. *Sky condition*—reported in the following format: Amount/Height/Type (as required) or Indefinite Ceiling/Height (Vertical Visibility)

j. *Temperature/dew point group*—two-digit form in whole degrees Celsius separated by a solidus (/). Temperatures below zero are prefixed with M.

k. *Altimeter*—four-digit format representing tens, units, tenths, and hundredths of inches of mercury prefixed with an "A." The decimal point is not reported or stated.

Continued

l. *Remarks (RMK) (as required)*—operational significant weather phenomena, location of phenomena, beginning and ending times, direction of movement.

Example: METAR KLAX 140651Z AUTO 00000KT 1SM
           R35L/4500V6000FT -RA BR BKN030 10/10 A2990
           RMK AO2

The following is an example of the phraseology used to relay this report to a pilot. Optional words or phrases are shown in parentheses: Los Angeles (California) (zero six five one observation), wind calm, visibility one, runway three five left RVR, variable between four thousand five hundred and six thousand feet, light rain, mist, broken ceiling 3,000 feet, temperature ten, dew point ten, altimeter two niner niner zero.

3. What are several types of weather observing programs? (AIM 7-1-12)

a. *Manual observations*—Reports made from airport locations staffed by FAA or NWS personnel.

b. *AWOS*—Automated Weather Observing System, which consists of various sensors, a processor, a computer-generated voice sub-system, and a transmitter to broadcast local, minute-by-minute weather data directly to the pilot. Observations include the prefix "AUTO" in the data.

c. *AWOS Broadcasts*—Computer-generated voice is used to automate the broadcast of minute-minute weather observations.

d. *ASOS/AWSS*—Automated Surface Observing System/Automated Weather Sensor System, the primary U.S. surface weather observing system. AWSS is a follow-on program that provides identical data as ASOS. The system provides continuous minute-by-minute observations generating METARs and other aviation weather information, transmitted over a discrete VHF radio frequency or the voice portion of a local NAVAID.

4. What are PIREPs (UA), and where are they usually found? (AC 00-45)

An abbreviation for "pilot weather reports." A report of meteorological phenomena encountered by aircraft in flight. Required elements for all PIREPs are: message type, location, time, altitude/flight level, type aircraft, and at least one other element to describe the reported phenomena. All altitude references are MSL unless otherwise noted. Distance for visibility is in SM; all other distances are in NM. Time is in UTC. The two types of PIREPs are the routine (UA) and the urgent (UUA).

5. What are radar weather reports? (AC 00-45)

A radar weather report (SD/ROB) contains information about precipitation observed by weather radar. It is a textual product derived from the WSR-88D NEXRAD radar without human intervention. Reports are transmitted hourly and contain the following: location ID, time, configuration (CELL, LN, and AREA), coverage, precipitation type and intensity, location, maximum tops, cell movement, and remarks. The resolution of an SD/ROB is very coarse, up to 80 minutes old, and should only be used if no other radar information is available.

J. Aviation Weather Forecasts

1. What are terminal aerodrome forecasts (TAFs)? (AC 00-45, AIM 7-1-30)

It is a concise statement of the expected meteorological conditions within a 5 SM radius from the center of an airport's runway complex during a 24-hour time period. TAFs use the same weather code found in METAR weather reports, in the following format:

a. *Type of reports*—a routine forecast (TAF), an amended forecast (TAF AMD), or a corrected forecast (TAF COR).

b. *ICAO station identifier*—4-letter station identifiers.

c. *Date and time of origin*—the date and UTC for when the forecast was actually prepared, in ICAO format. Valid time, TEMPOs and PROBs are presented ddhh/ddhh, FROM groups are presented ddhhmm.

d. *Valid period date and time*—valid forecast period is a 2-digit date followed by the 2-digit beginning and 2-digit ending hours in UTC. Routine TAFs are valid for 24 hours and are issued four times daily at 0000Z, 0600Z, 1200Z, and 1800Z.

e. *Forecasts*—wind; visibility; significant and vicinity weather; cloud and vertical obscuration; non-convective low-level wind shear; forecast change indicators (FM, TEMPO and PROB).

Note: The TAF date and time format recently changed to conform to ICAO standards. This change provides 30-hour TAFs for 32 high-impact U.S. airports. The remainder of TAF reporting stations will continue with 24-hour forecasts. The date and time format of all TAFs changed to accommodate the extended TAF period as detailed in item c. above.

2. What is an aviation area forecast? (AC 00-45)

A forecast of visual meteorological conditions (VMC), clouds, and general weather conditions over an area the size of several states. Must be used along with inflight weather advisories to determine forecast enroute weather and to interpolate conditions at airports where no TAFs are issued, in order to understand the complete weather picture. FAs are issued 3 times a day by the Aviation Weather Center (AWC) for each of the 6 areas in the contiguous 48 states.

3. What Information is provided by an aviation area forecast? (AC 00-45)

Area forecasts (abbreviated "FA") are issued for the conterminous U.S. and cover the airspace between the surface and 45,000 feet AMSL. They include:

a. Synopsis: brief discussion of the synoptic weather affecting the FA area during the 18-hour valid period.

b. Clouds and weather: description of the clouds and weather for the first 12-hour period for each state or group of states, including:

   • Cloud amount (SCT, BKN or OVC) for clouds with bases higher than or equal to 1,000 feet AGL and below FL180,

   • Cloud bases and tops (AMSL) associated with the above,

   • Precipitation,

   • Visibilities between 3 to 5 SM and obstruction(s) to visibility,

   • Sustained surface winds 20 knots or greater.

c. 12- to 18-hour categorical outlook: IFR, marginal VFR (MVFR), or VFR, including expected precipitation and/or obstruction(s) to visibility.

4. What are In-flight Aviation Weather Advisories (WST, WS, WA)? (AIM 7-1-6)

Forecasts that advise enroute aircraft of development of potentially hazardous weather. All heights are referenced MSL, except in the case of ceilings (CIG) which indicates AGL. The advisories are of three types: convective SIGMET (WST), SIGMET (WS), and AIRMET (WA).

5. What is a convective SIGMET? (AIM 7-1-6)

A convective SIGMET (WST) implies severe or greater turbulence, severe icing and low-level wind shear. It may be issued for any convective situation which the forecaster feels is hazardous to all categories of aircraft. Convective SIGMET bulletins are issued for the Eastern (E), Central (C) and Western (W) United States (convective SIGMETs are not issued for Alaska or Hawaii). Bulletins are issued hourly at H+55. Special bulletins are issued at any time as required and updated at H+55. The text of the bulletin consists of either an observation and a forecast, or just a forecast, which is valid for up to 2 hours.

a. Severe thunderstorm due to:

- Surface winds greater than or equal to 50 knots
- Hail at the surface greater than or equal to ¾ inches in diameter
- Tornadoes

b. Embedded thunderstorms

c. A line of thunderstorms

d. Thunderstorms producing greater than or equal to heavy precipitation that affects 40 percent or more of an area at least 3,000 square miles.

6. What is a SIGMET? (AIM 7-1-6)

A SIGMET (WS) advises of non-convective weather that is potentially hazardous to all aircraft. SIGMETs are issued for the six areas corresponding to the FA areas. The maximum forecast period is four hours. In the conterminous United States, SIGMETs are issued when the following phenomena occur or are expected to occur:

a. Severe icing not associated with a thunderstorm.

b. Severe or extreme turbulence or clear air turbulence (CAT) not associated with thunderstorms.

c. Dust storms or sandstorms lowering surface or in-flight visibilities to below 3 miles.

d. Volcanic ash.

7. What is an AIRMET? (AIM 7-1-6)

AIRMETs (WAs) are advisories of significant weather phenomena but describe conditions at intensities lower than those which require the issuance of SIGMETs. AIRMETs are intended for dissemination to all pilots in the preflight and en route phase of flight to enhance safety. AIRMET information is available in two formats: text bulletins (WA) and graphics (G-AIRMET) and are issued on a scheduled basis every 6 hours beginning at 0245 UTC. Unscheduled updates and corrections are issued as necessary. AIRMETs contain details about IFR, extensive mountain obscuration, turbulence, strong surface winds, icing, and freezing levels.

8. What are the different types of AIRMETs? (AIM 7-1-6)

There are three AIRMETs—Sierra, Tango, and Zulu:

a. AIRMET Sierra describes IFR conditions and/or extensive mountain obscurations.

b. AIRMET Tango describes moderate turbulence, sustained surface winds of 30 knots or greater, and/or nonconvective low-level wind shear.

c. AIRMET Zulu describes moderate icing and provides freezing level heights.

9. What is a winds and temperatures aloft forecast (FB)? (AC 00-45)

Winds and temperature aloft forecasts are computer prepared forecasts of wind direction, wind speed, and temperature at specified times, altitudes, and locations. They are produced 4 times daily for specified locations in the continental United States, Hawaii, Alaska and coastal waters, and the western Pacific Ocean. Amendments are not issued to the forecasts. Wind forecasts are not issued for altitudes within 1,500 feet of a location's elevation.

Some of the features of FBs are:

a. Product header includes date and time observations collected, forecast valid date and time, and the time period during which the forecast is to be used.

Continued

    b. Altitudes up to 15,000 feet referenced to MSL; altitudes at or above 18,000 feet are references to flight levels (FL).

    c. Temperature indicated in degrees Celsius (two digits) for the levels from 6,000 through 24,000 feet. Above 24,000 feet, minus sign is omitted since temperatures are always negative at those altitudes. Temperature forecasts are not issued for altitudes within 2,500 feet of a location's elevation. Forecasts for intermediate levels are determined by interpolation.

    d. Wind direction indicated in tens of degrees (two digits) with reference to true north and wind speed is given in knots (two digits). Light and variable wind or wind speeds of less than 5 knots are expressed by 9900. Forecast wind speeds of 100 through 199 knots are indicated by subtracting 100 from the speed and adding 50 to the coded direction. For example, a forecast of 250 degrees, 145 knots, is encoded as 7545. Forecast wind speeds of 200 knots or greater are indicated as a forecast speed of 199 knots. For example, 7799 is decoded as 270 degrees at 199 knots or greater.

10. What valuable information can be determined from a winds and temperatures aloft forecast?

Most favorable altitude—based on winds and direction of flight.

Areas of possible icing—by noting air temperatures of +2°C to -20°C.

Temperature inversions—a temperature increase with altitude can mean a stable layer aloft reducing the chance for convective activity.

Turbulence—by observing abrupt changes in wind direction and speed at different altitudes.

11. What is a Center Weather Advisory (CWA)? (AC 00-45)

A Center Weather Advisory (CWA) is an aviation warning for use by aircrews to anticipate and avoid adverse weather conditions in the en route and terminal environments. This is not a flight planning product; instead it reflects current conditions expected at the time of issuance, and/or is a short-range forecast for conditions expected to begin within 2 hours from that time. CWAs are valid for a maximum of 2 hours. If conditions are expected to continue beyond that period, a statement will be included in the CWA.

K. Aviation Weather Charts

1. Give examples of weather charts you will use during the flight planning process. (AC 00-45)

a. Surface Analysis Chart

b. Weather Depiction Chart

c. Radar Summary Chart

d. Significant Weather Prognostic Chart

e. Short-Range Surface Prognostic Chart

f. Convective Outlook Chart

g. Constant Pressure Analysis Chart

h. Freezing Level Graphics

2. What is a surface analysis chart? (AC 00-45)

The surface analysis chart is a computer-prepared chart that covers the contiguous 48 states and adjacent areas. The chart is transmitted every three hours. The surface analysis chart provides a ready means of locating pressure systems and fronts. It also gives an overview of winds, temperatures and dew point temperatures at chart time. When using the chart, keep in mind that weather moves and conditions change. Using the surface analysis chart in conjunction with other information gives a more complete weather picture.

3. What information does a weather depiction chart provide? (AC 00-45)

This chart is computer-generated (with frontal analysis by an observer) from METAR reports, and gives a broad overview of the observed flying category conditions at the valid time of the chart. It begins at 01Z each day, is transmitted at 3-hours intervals, and is valid at the time of the plotted data. Observations reported by both manual and automated observation locations provide the following data: total sky cover, cloud height, weather and obstructions to visibility, visibility. The weather depiction chart is an ideal place to begin preparing for a weather briefing and flight planning. From this chart, one can get a "bird's-eye-view" of areas of favorable and adverse weather conditions for chart time.

4. Define the terms: LIFR, IFR, MVFR and VFR. (AIM 7-1-7)

LIFR   Low IFR: ceiling less than 500 feet and/or visibility less
than 1 mile

IFR   Ceiling 500 to less than 1,000 feet and/or visibility 1 to
less than 3 miles

MVFR   Marginal VFR: ceiling 1,000 to 3,000 feet and/or visibility 3 to 5 miles inclusive

VFR   Ceiling greater than 3,000 feet and visibility greater than
5 miles; includes sky clear

5. What are radar summary charts? (AC 00-45)

This chart is a computer-generated graphical display of a collection
of automated radar weather reports (SDs, or ROBs), displaying
areas of precipitation as well as information about type, intensity,
configuration, coverage, echo top, and cell movement of precipitation. Severe weather watches are plotted if they are in effect when
the chart is valid. It is available hourly with a valid time 35 minutes past each hour.

This chart aids in preflight planning by identifying general
areas and movement of precipitation and/or thunderstorms. It displays drops or ice particles of precipitation size only; it does not
display clouds and fog. Therefore, since the absence of echoes does
not guarantee clear weather, and cloud tops will most likely be
higher than the tops of the precipitation echoes detected by radar,
the radar summary chart must be used in conjunction with other
charts, reports, and forecasts for best effectiveness.

6. What are Short-Range Surface Prognostic charts? (AC 00-45)

Short-Range Surface Prognostic (Prog) Charts provide a forecast
of surface pressure systems, fronts and precipitation for a 2-day
period. The forecast area covers the 48-contiguous states, the
coastal waters and portions of adjacent countries. The forecasted
conditions are divided into four forecast periods, 12-, 24-, 36-, and
48-hours. Each chart depicts a "snapshot" of weather elements
expected at the specified valid time.

These charts can be used to obtain an overview of the progression of surface weather features during the next 48 hours.

7. Describe a U.S. Low-Level Significant Weather Prog chart. (AC 00-45)

The Low-Level Significant Weather (SIGWX) charts provide a forecast of aviation weather hazards and are primarily intended for use as guidance products for pre-flight briefings. The forecast domain covers the 48 contiguous states and the coastal waters for altitudes 24,000 feet MSL (Flight Level 240 or 400 millibars) and below. Each chart depicts a "snapshot" of weather expected at the specified valid time and depicts weather flying categories (IFR or MVFR), turbulence, and freezing levels. Icing is not specifically forecast. Two charts are issued (a 12-hour and a 24-hour prog) four times per day by the Aviation Weather Center (AWC).

8. Describe a Mid-Level Significant Weather (SIGWX) chart. (AC 00-45)

This chart provides a forecast and an overview of significant enroute weather phenomena over a range of flight levels from 10,000 feet MSL to FL450, and associated surface weather features. It is a "snapshot" of weather expected at the specified valid time and depicts numerous weather elements that can be hazardous to aviation. The AWC issues the 24-hour Mid-Level Significant Weather chart 4 times daily.

9. What information may be obtained from the U.S. High-Level Significant Weather Prog charts? (AC 00-45)

High-Level Significant Weather (SIGWX) charts provide a forecast of significant en route weather phenomena over a range of flight levels from FL250 to FL630, and associated surface weather features. Each chart depicts a "snap-shot" of weather expected at the specified valid time. Conditions routinely appearing on the chart are:

a. Thunderstorms and cumulonimbus clouds

b. Moderate or severe turbulence

c. Moderate or severe icing

d. Jet streams

e. Tropopause heights

f. Tropical cyclones

g. Severe squall lines

h. Volcanic eruption sites

i. Widespread sandstorms and dust storms

10. What is a convective outlook chart? (AC 00-45)

The convective outlook chart (AC), is a two-panel chart that forecasts general thunderstorm activity for the valid period of the
chart. ACs describe areas in which there is a risk of severe thunderstorms. Severe thunderstorm criteria include winds equal to
or greater than 50 knots at the surface or hail equal to or greater
than ¾ inch in diameter, or tornadoes. ACs are useful for planning
flights within the forecast period. Both panels of the convective
outlook chart qualify the risk of thunderstorm activity at three
levels (slight, moderate, and high), as well as areas of general
thunderstorm activity. The day-1 panel is issued five times daily,
starting a 0600Z and is valid from 1200Z that day until 1200Z the
day after. The day-2 chart is issued twice daily starting at 0830Z
standard time, and is valid from 1200Z following the original issue
of the day-1 chart until 1200Z of the next day.

11. What are constant pressure analysis charts? (AC 00-45)

Any surface of equal pressure in the atmosphere is a constant
pressure surface. A constant pressure analysis chart is an upper
air weather map where all information depicted is at the specified
pressure of the chart. From these charts, a pilot can approximate
the observed air temperature, wind, and temperature/dewpoint
spread along a proposed route. They also depict highs, lows,
troughs, and ridges aloft by the height contour patterns resembling
isobars on a surface map. Twice daily, five computer-prepared constant pressure charts are issued from observed data:

850 mb .... 5,000 ft
700 mb .... 10,000 ft
500 mb .... 18,000 ft
300 mb .... 30,000 ft
200 mb .... 39,000 ft

12. What significance do height contour lines have on a constant pressure chart? (AC 00-45)

Heights of the specified pressure for each station are analyzed through the use of solid lines called contours to give a height pattern. The contours depict highs, lows, troughs, and ridges aloft in the same manner as isobars on the surface chart. Also, closely-spaced contours mean strong winds, as do closely-spaced isobars.

13. What significance do isotherms have on a constant pressure chart? (AC 00-45)

Isotherms (dashed lines) drawn at 5°C-intervals show horizontal temperature variations at chart altitude. By inspecting isotherms, you can determine if your flight will be toward colder or warmer air. Subfreezing temperatures and a temperature/dewpoint spread of 5°C or less suggest possible icing.

14. What is the significance of the isotach lines on a constant pressure chart? (AC 00-45)

Isotachs are lines of constant wind speed analyzed on the 300 and 200 mb charts; they separate higher wind speeds from lower wind speeds and are used to map wind speed variations over a surface. Isotachs are drawn at 20-knot intervals and begin at 10 knots. Isotach gradients identify the magnitude of wind speed variations. Strong gradients are closely spaced isotachs and identify large wind speed variations. Weak gradients are loosely spaced isotachs and identify small wind speed variations. Zones of very strong winds are highlighted by hatches.

15. What information does a freezing level graphics chart provide? (AC 00-45)

Freezing level graphics are used to assess the lowest freezing level heights and their values relative to flight paths. The chart uses colors to represent the height in hundreds of feet above mean sea level (MSL) of the lowest freezing level(s). The initial analysis and 3-hour forecast graphics are updated hourly. The 6-, 9-, and 12-hour forecast graphics are updated every three hours.

16. What information can a pilot obtain from current and forecast icing products (CIP and FIP)? (AC 00-45)

Current Icing Product (CIP)—provides an hourly three-dimensional diagnosis of the icing environment; information is displayed on a suite of twelve graphics available for the 48 contiguous United States, much of Canada and Mexico, and their respective coastal waters. CIP is a supplementary weather product for enhanced situational awareness only. The CIP product suite is issued hourly 15 minutes after the hour by the Aviation Weather Center (AWC).

Forecast Icing Potential (FIP)—provides a three-dimensional forecast of icing potential (or likelihood) using numerical weather prediction model output. It may be used as a higher resolution supplement to AIRMETs and SIGMETs but is not a substitute for them. The forecast area covers the 48 contiguous states, much of Canada and Mexico, and their respective coastal waters. The FIP is issued every hour and generates an hourly forecast for 3 hours into the future.

Additional Study Questions

1. Do the regulations require an operative pitot heater or alternate static source for IFR flight? (14 CFR 91.205)

2. What is the function of the "Kollsman" window on the altimeter? (FAA-H-8083-15)

3. What is the definition of a "standard-rate turn"? (FAA-H-8083-15)

4. Discuss the various types of weather reports a pilot would use to determine enroute weather. (AC 00-45)

5. Where can a pilot find information on the altitudes of cloud-layer tops? (AC 00-45)

6. The ATIS broadcast wind direction and speed are given in what values: magnetic or true north; knots or mph? (AIM 4-1-13)

7. What are several examples of charts, reports and forecasts that would be useful in determining the potential for and location of thunderstorms along your route? (AC 00-45)

8. When considering potential alternate airports, must an airport have an instrument approach to be legal as an alternate? (14 CFR 91.169)

9. Not all airports can be used as alternate airports. Why? (FAA-H-8261-1)

Departure 2

A. Authority and Limitations of the Pilot

1. Discuss 14 CFR §91.3, "Responsibility and Authority of PIC." (14 CFR 91.3)

The pilot-in-command of an aircraft is directly responsible for, and is the final authority as to the operation of that aircraft.

2. What are the right-of-way rules pertaining to IFR flights? (14 CFR 91.113)

When weather conditions permit, regardless of whether an operation is under IFR or VFR, vigilance shall be maintained by each person operating an aircraft so as to see and avoid other aircraft.

3. What are the required reports for equipment malfunction under IFR in controlled airspace? (AIM 5-3-3)

You must report:

a. Any loss in controlled airspace of VOR, TACAN, ADF, or low-frequency navigation receiver capability.

b. GPS anomalies while using installed IFR-certified GPS/GNSS receivers.

c. Complete or partial loss of ILS receiver capability.

d. Impairment of air/ground communication capability.

e. Loss of any other equipment installed in the aircraft which may impair safety and/or the ability to operate under IFR.

B. Departure Clearance

1. How can your IFR clearance be obtained? (AIM 5-1-8)

a. At airports with an ATC tower in operation, clearances may be received from either ground control or a specific clearance delivery frequency when available.

b. For departures from airports without an operating control tower, or in an outlying area:

   • Clearances may be received over the radio through a RCO (remote communication outlet) or, in some cases, over the telephone.

   • In some areas, a clearance delivery frequency is available that is usable at different airports within a particular geographic area, for example, Class B airspace.

   • A clearance may be obtained over a GCO (Ground Communication Outlet), which is an unstaffed, remote-controlled ground-to-ground communication facility that provides pilots with the capability to contact ATC/FSS via VHF to a telephone connection.

   • If the above methods are not available, your clearance can be obtained from ARTCC once you are airborne, provided you remain VFR in Class E airspace.

The procedure may vary due to geographical features, weather conditions, and the complexity of the ATC system. To determine the most effective means of receiving an IFR clearance, pilots should ask an FSS briefer for the most appropriate means of obtaining their IFR clearance.

2. What does "cleared as filed" mean? (AIM 5-2-5)

ATC will issue an abbreviated IFR clearance based on the route of flight as filed in the IFR flight plan, provided the filed route can be approved with little or no revision.

3. **Which clearance items are given in an abbreviated IFR clearance?** (AIM 4-4-3 and 5-2-5)

C learance Limit (destination airport or fix)
R oute (initial heading)
A ltitude (initial altitude)
F requency (departure)
T ransponder (squawk code)

Note: ATC procedures now require the controller to state the DP name, the current number and the DP transition name after the phrase "Cleared to (destination) airport" and prior to the phrase, "then as filed," for ALL departure clearances when the DP or DP transition is to be flown.

4. **What does "clearance void time" mean?** (AIM 5-2-6)

When operating from an airport without a tower, a pilot may receive a clearance containing a provision that if the flight has not departed by a specific time, the clearance is void.

A pilot who does not depart prior to the clearance void time must advise ATC as soon as possible of his/her intentions. ATC will normally notify the pilot of the time allotted to notify ATC. This time cannot exceed 30 minutes.

5. **What is the purpose of the term "hold for release" when included in an IFR clearance?** (AIM 5-2-6)

ATC may issue "hold for release" instructions in a clearance to delay an aircraft's departure for traffic management reasons (weather, traffic volume, etc.). A pilot may not depart utilizing that IFR clearance until a release time or additional instructions are received from ATC.

C. Departure Procedures

1. What minimums are necessary for IFR takeoff under 14 CFR Part 91? Under 121, 125, 129, or 135? (14 CFR 91.175)

For 14 CFR Part 91, none. For aircraft operated under 14 CFR Parts 121, 125, 129, or 135, if takeoff minimums are not prescribed under Part 97 for a particular airport, the following minimums apply to takeoffs under IFR for aircraft operating under those parts:

a. For aircraft having two engines or less—
1 statute mile visibility.

b. For aircraft having more than two engines—
½ statute mile visibility.

2. What is considered "good operating practice" in determining takeoff minimums for IFR flight?

If an instrument approach procedure has been prescribed for that airport, use the minimums for that approach for takeoff. If no approach procedure is available, basic VFR minimums are recommended (1,000 feet and 3 miles).

3. What are DPs and why are they necessary? (AIM 5-2-8)

Departure procedures are preplanned IFR procedures that provide obstruction clearance from the terminal area to the appropriate enroute structure. The primary reason they are established is to provide obstacle clearance protection. Also, at busier airports, they increase efficiency and reduce communication and departure delays. Pilots operating under Part 91 are strongly encouraged to file and fly a DP at night, during marginal VMC and IMC, when one is available.

4. What are the two types of DPs? (AIM 5-2-8)

a. ODPs (Obstacle Departure Procedures)—printed either textually or graphically, provide obstruction clearance via the least onerous route from the terminal area to the appropriate en route structure. ODPs are recommended for obstruction clearance and may be flown without ATC clearance unless an alternate departure procedure (SID or radar vector) has been specifically assigned by ATC.

b. SIDs (Standard Instrument Departures)—always printed graphically. Standard Instrument Departures are air traffic control (ATC) procedures printed for pilot/controller use in graphic form to provide obstruction clearance and a transition from the terminal area to the appropriate en route structure. SIDs are primarily designed for system enhancement and to reduce pilot/controller workload. ATC clearance must be received prior to flying a SID.

5. What are the two types of SIDs? (FAA-H-8261-1)

SIDs are categorized by the type of navigation used to fly the departure, so they are considered either pilot navigation or vector SIDs:

Pilot navigation SIDs—designed to allow you to provide your own navigation with minimal radio communication. This type of procedure usually contains an initial set of departure instructions followed by one or more transition routes.

Vector SIDs—usually require ATC to provide radar vectors from just after takeoff (ROC is based on a climb to 400 feet above the DER elevation before making the initial turn) until reaching the assigned route or a fix depicted on the SID chart.

6. What criteria are used to provide obstruction clearance during departure? (AIM 5-2-8)

Unless specified otherwise, required obstacle clearance for all departures, including diverse, is based on the pilot crossing the departure end of the runway at least 35 feet above the departure end of runway elevation, climbing to 400 feet above the departure end of runway elevation before making the initial turn, and maintaining a minimum climb gradient of 200 feet per nautical mile (FPNM), unless required to level off by a crossing restriction, until the minimum IFR altitude. A greater climb gradient may be specified in the DP to clear obstacles or to achieve an ATC crossing restriction.

7. **Where are DPs located?** (AIM 5-2-8)

   DPs will be listed by airport in the IFR Takeoff Minimums and (Obstacle) Departure Procedures section, Section L, of the Terminal Procedures Publications (TPPs).

8. **Must you accept a SID if assigned one?** (FAA-H-8261-1)

   If you cannot comply with a SID, if you do not possess SID charts or textual descriptions, or if you simply do not wish to use standard instrument departures, include the statement "NO SIDs" in the remarks section of your flight plan.

9. **How does a pilot determine if takeoff minimums are not standard and/or departure procedures are published for an airport?** (FAA-H-8261-1)

   If an airport has non-standard takeoff minimums, a "triangle T" (or, "trouble T") symbol—that is, a black triangle with a T inside it—will be placed in the notes sections of the instrument procedure chart.

10. **Prior to departing an airport on an IFR flight, a pilot should determine whether they will be able to ensure adequate separation from terrain and obstacles. What information should this include?** (AIM 5-2-8)

    a. The type of terrain and other obstacles on or in the vicinity of the departure airport.

    b. Whether an ODP is available.

    c. If obstacle avoidance can be maintained visually or if the ODP should be flown.

    d. The effect of degraded climb performance and the actions to take in the event of an engine loss during the departure.

11. **If an ODP has been published for the runway you are departing from, are you required to follow it?** (FAA-H-8261-1)

    No; If they are not issued by ATC, textual ODPs are at the pilot's option to fly or not fly, even in less-than-VFR weather conditions for Part 91 operators, military, and public service.

12. When a DP specifies a climb gradient in excess of 200 feet per nautical mile, what significance should this have to the pilot? (AIM 5-2-8)

If an aircraft may turn in any direction from a runway, and remain clear of obstacles, that runway passes what is called diverse departure criteria and no ODP will be published. A SID may be published if needed for air traffic control purposes. However, if an obstacle penetrates what is called the 40:1 slope obstacle identification surface, then the procedure designer chooses whether to:

a. Establish a steeper than normal climb gradient; or

b. Establish a steeper than normal climb gradient with an alternative that increases takeoff minima to allow the pilot to visually remain clear of the obstacle(s); or

c. Design and publish a specific departure route; or

d. A combination or all of the above.

13. A climb gradient of 300 feet per nautical mile at a ground speed of 100 knots requires what rate of climb? (Terminal Procedures Rate of Climb/Descent Table)

Ground speed divided by 60 minutes times climb gradient = feet per minute; therefore,

$$\frac{100}{60} \times 300 = 500 \text{ feet per minute}$$

14. What is the recommended climb rate procedure, when issued a climb to an assigned altitude by ATC? (AIM 4-4-10)

When ATC has not used the term "At Pilot's Discretion" nor imposed any climb or descent restrictions, pilots should initiate climb or descent promptly on acknowledgement of the clearance. Descend or climb at an optimum rate consistent with the operating characteristics of the aircraft to 1,000 feet above or below the assigned altitude, and then attempt to descend or climb at a rate of between 500 and 1,500 fpm until the assigned altitude is reached.

15. All public RNAV SIDs and graphic ODPs are RNAV1. What does this mean? (AIM 5-2-8; AC 90-100)

RNAV 1 terminal procedures require that the aircraft's track keeping accuracy remain bound by +1 nautical mile (NM) for 95 percent of the total flight time. All pilots are expected to maintain route centerlines, as depicted by onboard lateral deviation indicators and/or flight guidance during all RNAV operations unless authorized to deviate by ATC or under emergency conditions.

D. VOR Accuracy Checks

1. What are the different methods for checking the accuracy of VOR equipment? (14 CFR 91.171)

a. VOR test signal (VOT) check: ±4°; or

b. Radio repair station test signal: ±4°; or

c. VOR ground checkpoint at departure airport: ±4°; or

d. VOR airborne checkpoint: ±6° (if no test signal or ground checkpoint available); or

e. Airborne over prominent landmark along centerline of established VOR airway (more than 20 NM from VOR): ±6° (if no check signal or point is available).

f. Dual VOR system check by checking one system against the other; both systems tuned to same VOR and note the indicated bearings to station; maximum permissible variation between the two indicated bearings is 4°. The dual system check can be used in place of all other VOR check procedures specified.

Note: A repair station can use a radiated test signal, but only the technician performing the test can make an entry in the logbook.

2. What records must be kept concerning VOR checks? (14 CFR 91.171)

Each person making a VOR check shall enter the date, place and bearing error, and sign the aircraft log or other reliable record.

3. Where can a pilot find the location of airborne checkpoints, ground checkpoints and VOT testing stations? (AIM 1-1-4)

Locations of airborne checkpoints, ground checkpoints, and VOTs are published in the A/FD.

4. What procedure is used when checking VOR receiver accuracy with a VOT? (FAA-H-8083-15)

Tune in the VOT frequency of 108.0 MHz. With CDI centered, the OBS should read 0 degrees with TO/FROM indication showing FROM or the OBS should read 180 degrees with the TO/FROM indication showing TO.

Remember: "Cessna 182"—180 TO for VOR accuracy checks using a VOT.

E. Transponder

1. Where is altitude encoding transponder equipment required? (AIM 4-1-20)

In general, the regulations require aircraft to be equipped with Mode C transponders when operating:

a. At or above 10,000 feet MSL over the 48 contiguous states or the District of Columbia, excluding that airspace below 2,500 feet AGL;

b. Within 30 miles of a Class B airspace primary airport, below 10,000 feet MSL;

c. Within and above all Class C airspace, up to 10,000 feet MSL;

d. Within 10 miles of certain designated airports, excluding that airspace which is both outside the Class D surface area and below 1,200 feet AGL;

e. All aircraft flying into, within, or across the contiguous United States ADIZ.

Note: Civil and military transponders should be turned to the "On" or normal altitude reporting position prior to moving on the airport surface to ensure the aircraft is visible to ATC surveillance systems.

2. **What are the following transponder codes?** (AIM 4-1-20, 6-2-2, 6-3-4, and 6-4-2)

1200 .... VFR
7700 .... Emergency
7600 .... Communications Emergency
7500 .... Hijacking in progress

3. **Discuss transponder operation in the event of a two-way communications failure.** (AIM 6-4-2)

If an aircraft with a coded radar beacon transponder experiences a loss of two-way radio capability, the pilot should adjust the transponder to reply on Mode A/3, Code 7600.

Note: The pilot should understand that the aircraft might not be in an area of radar coverage.

4. **Would an incorrect altimeter setting have an effect on the Mode C altitude information transmitted by your transponder?** (AIM 4-1-20)

No. While an incorrect altimeter setting has no effect on the Mode C altitude information transmitted by your transponder (transponders are preset at 29.92), it would cause you to fly at an actual altitude different from your assigned altitude.

When a controller indicates that an altitude readout is invalid, the pilot should initiate a check to verify that the aircraft altimeter is set correctly.

F. Airport Facilities

1. **Where can a pilot find information concerning facilities available for a particular airport?** (AIM 9-1-4)

In the *Airport/Facility Directory*; it contains information concerning services available, communication data, navigational facilities, special notices, etc. The A/FD is reissued in its entirety every 56 days.

2. What do the following acronyms stand for? (AIM 2-1-1, 2-1-2, and 2-1-3)

ALS.. Approach Light System

VASI.. Visual Approach Slope Indicator

PAPI.. Precision Approach Path Indicator

REIL .... Runway End Identifier Lights

3. What color are runway edge lights? (AIM 2-1-4)

The runway edge lights are white—except on instrument runways, yellow replaces white on the last 2,000 feet or half the runway length, whichever is less, to form a caution zone for landings.

4. What colors and color combinations are standard airport rotating beacons? (AIM 2-1-10)

Lighted Land Airport .... White/Green

Lighted Water Airport .... White/Yellow

Military Airport.............................. 2 White/Green

5. What does the operation of a rotating beacon at an airport within Class D airspace during daylight hours mean? (AIM 2-1-10)

In Class B, Class C, Class D, and Class E surface areas, operation of the airport beacon during the hours of daylight often indicates that the ground visibility is less than 3 miles and/or the ceiling is less than 1,000 feet. ATC clearance in accordance with 14 CFR Part 91 is required for landing, takeoff and flight in the traffic pattern. Pilots should not rely solely on the operation of the airport beacon to indicate if weather conditions are IFR or VFR. There is no regulatory requirement for daylight operation and it is the pilot's responsibility to comply with proper preflight planning as required by 14 CFR Part 91.

6. Where would information concerning runway lengths, widths and weight bearing capacities be found? (A/FD)

The *Airport/Facility Directory* has this information.

7. What are runway touchdown zone markings? (AIM 2-3-3)

Touchdown zone markings identify the touchdown zone for landing operations and are coded to provide distance information in 500-foot increments. These markings consist of groups of one, two, and three rectangular bars symmetrically arranged in pairs about the runway centerline. Normally, the standard glide slope angle of 3 degrees, if flown to the surface, will ensure touchdown within this zone.

8. What is the purpose of runway aiming point markings? (AIM 2-3-3)

The aiming point markings serve as a visual aiming point for a landing aircraft. These two rectangular markings consist of a broad white stripe, located on each side of the runway centerline, and approximately 1,000 feet from the landing threshold. The pilot can estimate a visual glide path that will intersect the marking ensuring a landing within the 3,000-foot touchdown zone.

9. How far down a runway does the touchdown zone extend? (P/CG)

The touchdown zone is the first 3,000 feet of the runway beginning at the threshold. The area is used for determination of Touchdown Zone Elevation in the development of straight-in landing minimums for instrument approaches.

10. How can you identify an ILS critical area? (AIM 1-1-9)

Holding position markings for ILS critical areas consist of two yellow solid lines, spaced two feet apart, connected by pairs of solid lines, spaced ten feet apart, extending across the width of the taxiway. When the ILS critical area is being protected, the pilot should stop so no part of the aircraft extends beyond the holding position marking. The area is protected whenever conditions are less than a ceiling of 800 feet and/or visibility less than 2 miles.

11. What does the acronym "RWSL" stand for? (AIM 2-1-6)

Runway Status Lights system—a fully automated system that provides runway status information to pilots and surface vehicle operators to clearly indicate when it is unsafe to enter, cross, takeoff from, or land on a runway. The RWSL system processes information from surveillance systems and activates Runway Entrance Lights (REL), Takeoff Hold Lights (THL), Runway Intersection Lights (RIL), and Final Approach Runway Occupancy Signal (FAROS) in accordance with the position and velocity of the detected surface traffic and approach traffic. The status lights have two states—ON: lights are illuminated red; and OFF: lights are not illuminated.

12. Describe runway hold short markings and signs. (AIM 2-3-5)

Runway holding position markings—indicate where an aircraft is supposed to stop when approaching a runway. They consist of four yellow lines—two solid and two dashed—spaced six or twelve inches apart and extending across the width of the taxiway or runway. The solid lines are always on the side where the aircraft is to hold.

Runway holding position sign—located at the holding position on taxiways that intersect a runway or on runways that intersect other runways. These signs have a red background with a white inscription and contain the designation of the intersecting runway.

13. **Pre-flight planning for taxi operations should be an integral part of the pilot's flight planning process. What information should this include?** (AC 91-73)

    a. Review and understand airport signage, markings and lighting.

    b. Review the airport diagram, planned taxi route, and identify any "hot spots."

    c. Review the latest airfield NOTAMs and ATIS (if available) for taxiway/runway closures, construction activity, etc.

    d. Conduct a pre-taxi/pre-landing briefing that includes the expected/assigned taxi route, any hold short lines and restrictions based on ATIS information or previous experience at the airport.

    e. Plan for critical times and locations on the taxi route (complex intersections, crossing runways, etc.).

    f. Plan to complete as many aircraft checklist items as possible prior to taxi.

14. **What is an airport surface "hot spot"?** (A/FD)

    A "hot spot" is a runway safety-related problem area on an airport that presents increased risk during surface operations. Typically, hot spots are complex or confusing taxiway–taxiway or taxiway–runway intersections. The area of increased risk has either a history of or potential for runway incursions or surface incidents due to a variety of causes, such as but not limited to: airport layout, traffic flow, airport marking, signage and lighting, situational awareness, and training. Hot spots are depicted on airport diagrams as circles or polygons designated as "HS1", "HS2", etc.

15. When issued taxi instructions to an assigned takeoff runway, are you automatically authorized to cross any runway that intersects your taxi route? (AIM 4-3-18)

No; Aircraft must receive a runway crossing clearance for each runway that their taxi route crosses. When assigned a takeoff runway, ATC will first specify the runway, issue taxi instructions, and state any hold short instructions or runway crossing clearances if the taxi route will cross a runway. When issuing taxi instructions to any point other than an assigned takeoff runway, ATC will specify the point to which to taxi, issue taxi instructions, and state any hold short instructions or runway crossing clearances if the taxi route will cross a runway. ATC is required to obtain from the pilot a readback of all runway hold short instructions.

16. How can a pilot maintain situational awareness during taxi operations? (AC 91-73)

a. Ensure that a current airport diagram is available for immediate reference during taxi.

b. Monitor ATC instructions/clearances issued to other aircraft for the "big picture."

c. Focus attention outside the cockpit while taxiing.

d. Use all available resources (airport diagrams, airport signs, markings, lighting, and ATC) to keep the aircraft on its assigned taxi route.

e. Cross-reference heading indicator to ensure turns are being made in the correct direction and that you're on the assigned taxi route.

f. Prior to crossing any hold short line, visually check for conflicting traffic; verbalize "clear left, clear right."

g. Be alert for other aircraft with similar call signs on the frequency.

h. Understand and follow all ATC instructions and if in doubt—ask!

Additional Study Questions

1. What are pre-taxi clearance procedures? How do you determine if they are available? (AIM 5-2-1)

2. What responsibilities does a pilot have concerning readback of ATC clearances and instructions? (AIM 4-4-7)

3. Is an ATC clearance an authorization for a pilot to deviate from any rule, regulation or minimum altitude? (AIM 4-4-1)

4. ATC may issue a "release" time to an IFR flight. What significance does this have? (AIM 5-2-6)

5. What procedures should be used to determine that ADF equipment in the aircraft is functional? (FAA-H-8083-15)

6. What is the difference between a VFR Over-The-Top clearance and a VFR-On-Top clearance? (FAA-H-8083-15)

7. What does the term "radar contact" mean when used by the controller during a departure? Who is responsible for terrain and obstacle clearance? (AIM 5-2-8)

En Route

3

A. Enroute Limitations

1. Define the following. (P/CG)

MEA   Minimum Enroute Altitude; the lowest published altitude between radio fixes that ensures acceptable navigational signal coverage and meets obstacle clearance requirements.

MOCA—Minimum Obstruction Clearance Altitude; the lowest published altitude between radio fixes on VOR airways, off-airway routes, or route segments that meets obstacle clearance requirements, and that ensures acceptable navigational signal coverage only within 25 statute (22 nautical) miles of a VOR.

MCA—Minimum Crossing Altitude; the lowest altitude at certain fixes at which aircraft must cross when proceeding in the direction of a higher MEA.

MRA—Minimum Reception Altitude; the lowest altitude at which an intersection can be determined.

MAA—Maximum Authorized Altitude; the maximum usable altitude or flight level for an airspace structure or a route segment that ensures adequate reception of navigation aid signals.

OROCA—Off-Route Obstruction Clearance Altitude; this provides obstruction clearance with a 1,000-foot buffer in non-mountainous terrain areas and a 2,000-foot buffer in designated mountainous areas within the United States. This altitude might not provide signal coverage from ground-based navigational aids, Air Traffic Control radar, or communications coverage.

2. If no applicable minimum altitude is prescribed (no MEA or MOCA), what minimum altitudes apply for IFR operations? (14 CFR 91.177 and Part 95)

Minimum altitudes are:

a. Mountainous terrain—at least 2,000 feet above the highest obstacle within a horizontal distance of 4 NM from the course to be flown. Part 95 designates the location of mountainous terrain.

b. Other than mountainous terrain—at least 1,000 feet above the highest obstacle within a horizontal distance of 4 NM from the course to be flown.

3. What cruising altitudes shall be maintained while operating under IFR in controlled airspace (Class A, B, C, D, or E)? In uncontrolled airspace (Class G)? (14 CFR 91.179)

IFR flights within controlled airspace (Class A, B, C, D, or E) shall maintain the altitude or flight level assigned by ATC. In uncontrolled airspace (Class G), altitude is selected based on the magnetic course flown:

Below 18,000 feet MSL:

0 to 179° .... odd thousand MSL
180 to 359° .... even thousand MSL

18,000 feet up to but not including 29,000 feet MSL:

0 to 179° .... odd flight levels
180 to 359° .... even flight levels

4. What procedures are applicable concerning courses to be flown when operating IFR? (14 CFR 91.181)

Unless otherwise authorized by ATC, no one may operate an aircraft within controlled airspace under IFR except on an air traffic services (ATS) route, along the centerline of that airway, or on any other route along the direct course between the navigational aids or fixes defining that route. However, this does not prohibit maneuvering the aircraft to pass well clear of other air traffic, or maneuvering in VFR conditions to clear the intended flight path both before and during climb or descent.

5. On a direct flight not flown on radials or courses of established airways or routes, what points serve as compulsory reporting points? (AIM 5-3-2)

For flights along a direct route, regardless of the altitude or flight level being flown, including flights operating in accordance with an ATC clearance specifying "VFR-On-Top," pilots must report over each reporting point used in the flight plan to define the route of flight.

6. What are "unpublished" RNAV routes? (AIM 5-3-4)

Unpublished RNAV routes are direct routes based on area navigation capability, between waypoints defined in terms of latitude/
longitude coordinates, degree distance fixes, or offsets from estab
lished routes/airways at a specified distance and direction. Radar
monitoring by ATC is required on all unpublished RNAV routes.

B. Enroute Procedures

1. What reports should be made to ATC at all times without a specific request? (AIM 5-3-3)

The pilot must report:

a. When vacating any previously assigned altitude or flight level
for a newly assigned altitude or flight level.

b. When an altitude change will be made if operating on a clearance specifying VFR-On-Top.

c. When unable to climb/descend at a rate of at least 500 feet per
minute.

d. When approach has been missed (request clearance for specific
action; i.e., to alternate airport, another approach, etc.).

e. Change in the average true speed (at cruising altitude) when it
varies by 5 percent or 10 knots (whichever is greater) from that
filed in the flight plan.

f. The time and altitude or flight level upon reaching a holding fix
or point that the pilot is cleared to.

g. When leaving any assigned holding fix or point.

h. Any loss, in controlled airspace, of VOR, TACAN, ADF, low-
frequency navigation receiver capability, GPS anomalies while
using installed IFR-certified GPS/GNSS receivers, complete
or partial loss of ILS receiver capability or impairment of
air/ground communications capability.

i. Any information relating to the safety of flight.

j. Upon encountering weather conditions which have not been
forecast, or hazardous conditions which have been forecast.

2. **What reporting requirements are required by ATC when not in radar contact?** (AIM 5-3-3)

   a. When leaving final approach fix inbound on the final (nonprecision) approach, or when leaving the outer marker (or fix used in lieu of the outer marker) inbound on final (precision) approach.

   b. A corrected estimate at anytime it becomes apparent that an estimate as previously submitted is in error in excess of 3 minutes.

3. **What items of information should be included in every position report?** (AIM 5-3-2)

   a. Identification

   b. Position

   c. Time

   d. Altitude or flight level

   e. Type of flight plan (not required in IFR position reports made directly to ARTCCs or approach control)

   f. ETA and name of next reporting point

   g. The name only of the next succeeding reporting point along the route of flight, and

   h. Pertinent remarks

4. **When used in conjunction with ATC altitude assignments, what does the term "pilot's discretion" mean?** (AIM Glossary)

   Pilot's discretion means that ATC has offered the pilot the option of starting climb or descent whenever he/she wishes and conducting the climb or descent at any rate he/she wishes. The pilot may temporarily level off at any intermediate altitude. However, after vacating an altitude, the pilot may not return to that altitude.

5. Explain the terms "maintain" and "cruise" as they pertain to an IFR altitude assignment. (AIM 4-4-3)

Maintain—Self-explanatory: maintain last altitude assigned.

Cruise—Used instead of "maintain" to assign a block of airspace to a pilot, from minimum IFR altitude up to and including the altitude specified in the cruise clearance. The pilot may level off at any intermediate altitude, and climb/descent may be made at the discretion of the pilot. However, once the pilot starts a descent, and *verbally* reports leaving an altitude in the block, he may not return to that altitude without additional ATC clearance.

6. Can a cruise clearance authorize you to execute an approach at the destination airport? (FAA-H-8261-1)

Yes. ATC may issue a cruise clearance that authorizes you to execute an approach upon arrival at the destination airport. When operating in uncontrolled airspace on a cruise clearance, you are responsible for determining the minimum IFR altitude. In addition, descent and landing at an airport in uncontrolled airspace are governed by the applicable visual flight rules and/or operations specifications, i.e. 14 CFR §91.126, 91.155, 91.175, 91.179, etc.

7. Why would a pilot request a VFR-On-Top clearance? (AIM 4-4-8)

A pilot on an IFR flight plan operating in VFR weather conditions, may request VFR-On-Top in lieu of an assigned altitude. For reasons such as turbulence, more favorable winds aloft, etc., the pilot has the flexibility to select an altitude or flight level of his/her choice (subject to any ATC restrictions). Pilots desiring to climb through a cloud, haze, smoke, or other meteorological formation and then either cancel their IFR flight plan or operate VFR-On-Top may request a climb to VFR-On-Top.

Note: The ATC authorization must contain either a top report or a statement that no top report is available, and a request to report reaching VFR-On-Top. Additionally, the ATC authorization may contain a clearance limit, routing, and an alternative clearance if VFR-On-Top is not reached by a specified altitude.

8. Does an ATC authorization to "maintain VFR-On-Top" restrict you to only operating on top or above the cloud layer? (AIM 4-4-8)

ATC authorization to "maintain VFR-On-Top" is not intended to restrict pilots so that they must operate only above an obscuring meteorological formation (layer). Instead, it permits operation above, below, between layers, or in areas where there is no meteorological obscuration. It is imperative, however, that pilots understand that clearance to operate "VFR-On-Top/VFR conditions" does not imply cancellation of the IFR flight plan.

9. Which airspace prohibits VFR-On-Top clearances? (AIM 4-4-8)

Class A airspace.

10. What operational procedures must pilots on IFR flight plans adhere to when operating VFR-On-Top? (AIM 4-4-8)

They must:

a. Fly at the appropriate VFR altitude

b. Comply with the VFR visibility and distance from cloud criteria

c. Comply with instrument flight rules that are applicable to this flight; i.e., minimum IFR altitudes, position reporting, radio communications, course to be flown, adherence to ATC clearance, etc.

11. What is a "clearance limit" and when is it received? (AIM 4-4-3)

A traffic clearance issued prior to departure will normally authorize flight to the airport of intended landing. Under certain conditions, at some locations, a short-range clearance procedure is used, whereby a clearance is issued to a fix within or just outside of the terminal area, and pilots are advised of the frequency on which they will receive the long-range clearance direct from the center controller.

12. What information will ATC provide when they request a hold at a fix where the holding pattern is not charted? (AIM 5-3-8)

An ATC clearance requiring an aircraft to hold at a fix where the pattern is not charted will include the following information:

a. Direction of holding from the fix, in reference to the eight cardinal compass points (i.e. N, NE, E, SE, etc.).

b. Holding fix (the fix may be omitted if included at the beginning of the transmission as the clearance limit).

c. Radial, course, bearing, airway or route on which the aircraft is to hold.

d. Leg length in miles if DME or RNAV is to be used (leg length will be specified in minutes on pilot request or if the controller considers it necessary).

e. Direction of turns, if holding pattern is nonstandard (left turns), the pilot requests direction of turns, or the controller considers it necessary to state direction of turns.

f. Time to expect further clearance and any pertinent additional delay information.

13. What are the maximum airspeeds permitted for aircraft while holding? (AIM 5-3-8)

MHA–6,000 ft .... 200 KIAS
6,001–14,000 ft .... 230 KIAS
14,001 and above .... 265 KIAS

Note: Holding patterns may be restricted to a maximum speed. Holding patterns from 6,001 to 14,000 feet may be restricted to a maximum airspeed of 210 KIAS. These nonstandard patterns will be depicted by an icon.

14. What is a nonstandard versus a standard holding pattern? (AIM 5-3-8)

In a standard pattern, all turns are to the right. In a nonstandard pattern, all turns are to the left.

15. Describe the procedure for crosswind correction in a holding pattern. (AIM 5-3-8)

Compensate for wind effect primarily by drift correction on the inbound and outbound legs. When outbound, triple the inbound drift correction to avoid major turning adjustments.

16. What action is appropriate when approaching a holding fix at an airspeed in excess of maximum holding speed? (AIM 5-3-8)

Start a speed reduction when 3 minutes or less from the fix. Speed may be reduced earlier, but ATC must be advised of the change.

17. Why is it important for the pilot to receive an EFC time with initial holding instructions? (FAA-H-8261-1)

If you lose two-way radio communication, the EFC allows you to depart the holding fix at a definite time. Plan the last lap of your holding pattern to leave the fix as close as possible to the exact time.

18. Describe the different recommended entry methods for holding. (AIM 5-3-8)

The three types of entry are:

a. Parallel
b. Teardrop
c. Direct

19. What is the leg length for a standard holding pattern? (AIM 5-3-8)

The standard leg length is:

a. 1 minute inbound at or below 14,000 feet MSL, and

b. 1½ minutes inbound above 14,000 feet MSL.

20. If assigned a DME/GPS hold, what procedures should be used? (AIM 5-3-8)

Distance Measuring Equipment (DME)/GPS Along-Track Distance (ATD) holding is subject to the same entry and holding procedures except that distances (nautical miles) are used in lieu of time values. The outbound course of the DME/GPS holding pattern is called the outbound leg of the pattern. The controller or the instrument approach procedure chart will specify the length of the outbound leg. The end of the outbound leg is determined by the DME or ATD readout.

21. When does the timing for the outbound leg in a holding pattern begin? (AIM 5-3-8)

Outbound leg timing begins over/abeam the fix, whichever occurs later. If the abeam position cannot be determined, start timing when turn to outbound is completed.

C. Oxygen Requirements

1. What regulations apply concerning supplemental oxygen? (14 CFR 91.211)

a. At cabin pressure altitudes above 12,500 MSL up to and including 14,000 MSL, the minimum flight crew must use oxygen after 30 minutes.

b. Above 14,000 MSL up to and including 15,000 MSL, the minimum flight crew must continuously use oxygen.

c. Above 15,000 MSL, each passenger must be provided with supplemental oxygen and the minimum flight crew must continuously use oxygen.

D. Emergencies

1. **When may the pilot-in-command of an aircraft deviate from an ATC clearance?** (14 CFR 91.123)

   Except in an emergency, no person may, in an area in which air traffic control is exercised, operate an aircraft contrary to an ATC instruction.

2. **If an emergency action requires deviation from 14 CFR Part 91, must a pilot submit a written report, and if so, to whom?** (14 CFR 91.123)

   Each pilot-in-command who is given priority by ATC in an emergency shall, if requested by ATC, submit a detailed report of that emergency within 48 hours to the manager of that ATC facility.

3. **Concerning two-way radio communications failure in VFR and IFR conditions, what is the procedure for altitude, route, leaving holding fix, descent for approach, and approach selection?** (14 CFR 91.185)

   In VFR conditions: If the failure occurs in VFR, or if VFR is encountered after the failure, each pilot shall continue the flight under VFR and land as soon as practicable.

   In IFR conditions: If the failure occurs in IFR conditions, or if VFR conditions are not within range, each pilot shall continue the flight according to the following:

   a. Route:

   A ssigned.......... by route assigned in last ATC clearance

   V ectored.......... go direct from point of radio failure to fix, route, airway in vector clearance

   E xpected........ by route that ATC has advised may be expected

   F iled .... by the route filed in flight plan

b. Altitude (highest of following altitudes for the route segment being flown):

   Minimum......... minimum altitude for IFR operations

   E xpected......... altitude/flight level ATC has advised to expect in a further clearance

   A ssigned.......... altitude/flight level assigned in the last ATC clearance

c. Leave clearance limit:

   • When the clearance limit is a fix from which the approach begins, commence descent or descent and approach as close as possible to the expect-further-clearance time if one has been received; or if one has not been received, as close as possible to the estimated time of arrival as calculated from the filed or amended (with ATC) estimated time en route.

   • If the clearance limit is not a fix from which the approach begins, leave the clearance limit at the expect-further-clearance time if one has been received; or if none has been received, upon arrival over the clearance limit, and proceed to a fix from which an approach begins and commence descent or decent and approach as close as possible to the estimated time of arrival as calculated from the filed or amended (with ATC) estimated time en route.

4. **Assuming two-way communications failure, discuss the recommended procedure to follow concerning altitudes to be flown for the following trip:**

   The MEA between A and B is 5,000 feet; the MEA between B and C is 5,000 feet; the MEA between C and D is 11,000 feet; and the MEA between D and E is 7,000 feet. You have been cleared via A, B, C, D, to E. While flying between A and B, your assigned altitude was 6,000 feet and you were told to expect a clearance to 8,000 feet at B. Prior to receiving the higher altitude assignment, you experience two-way communication failure. (AIM 6-4-1)

   The correct procedure would be as follows:

   a. Maintain 6,000 feet to B, then climb to 8,000 feet (the altitude you were advised to expect).

   b. Continue to maintain 8,000 feet, then climb to 11,000 feet at C, or prior to C if necessary to comply with an MCA at C.

   c. Upon reaching D, you would descend to 8,000 feet (even though the MEA was 7,000 feet), as 8,000 feet was the highest of the altitude situations stated in the rule.

5. **Assuming two-way communications failure, discuss the recommended procedure to follow concerning altitudes to be flown for the following scenario:**

   A pilot experiencing two-way radio failure while being progressively descended to lower altitudes to begin an approach is assigned 2,700 feet until crossing the VOR and then cleared for the approach. The MOCA along the airway is 2,700 feet and MEA is 4,000 feet. The aircraft is within 22 NM of the VOR. (AIM 6-4-1)

   The pilot should remain at 2,700 feet until crossing the VOR because that altitude is the minimum IFR altitude for the route segment being flown.

6. If you become doubtful about your position or adverse weather ahead, should you declare an emergency? (AIM 6-1-2)

An emergency can be either a distress or urgency condition. Pilots do not hesitate to declare an emergency when they are faced with distress conditions such as fire, mechanical failure, or structural damage. However, some are reluctant to report an urgency condition when they encounter situations that may not be immediately perilous, but are potentially catastrophic. An aircraft is in at least an urgency condition the moment the pilot becomes doubtful about position, fuel endurance, weather, or any other condition that could adversely affect flight safety. This is the time to ask for help, not after the situation has developed into a distress condition.

E. Single-Pilot Resource Management

1. Define the term "single-pilot resource management." (FAA-S-8081-4)

Single-pilot resource management (SRM) is defined as the art and science of managing all the resources (both on-board the aircraft and from outside sources) available to a single pilot (prior to and during flight) to ensure the successful outcome of the flight.

2. What are the various resources you will use when utilizing your SRM skills? (FAA-S-8081-4)

SRM available resources can include human resources, hardware, and information. Human resources include all other groups routinely working with the pilot who are involved in decisions required to operate a flight safely. These groups include, but are not limited to: dispatchers, weather briefers, maintenance personnel, and air traffic controllers. SRM is a set of skill competencies that must be evident in all Tasks required by the practical test standards as applied to single-pilot operation.

3. **What are the six skills you must be competent in for effective SRM?** (FAA-H-8083-25)

   C ontrolled Flight Into Terrain Awareness
   A eronautical Decision Making
   R isk Management
   A utomation Management
   T ask Management
   S ituational Awareness

4. **Define the term "aeronautical decision making."** (FAA-H-8083-9)

   Aeronautical decision making (ADM) is a systematic approach to the mental process used by aircraft pilots to consistently determine the best course of action in response to a given set of circumstances.

5. **The DECIDE model of decision making involves which elements?** (FAA-H-8083-9)

   D etect a change needing attention.
   E stimate the need to counter or react to the change.
   C hoose the most desirable outcome for the flight.
   I dentify actions to successfully control the change.
   D o something to adapt to the change.
   E valuate the effect of the action countering the change.

6. **What practical application provides a pilot with an effective method to utilize SRM?** (FAA-H-8083-2)

   The "Five P" checklist consists of "the Plan, the Plane, the Pilot, the Passengers, and the Programming." It is based on the idea that pilots have essentially five variables that impact their environment and can cause a pilot to make a single critical decision, or make several less critical decisions that when added together can create a critical outcome.

7. Explain the use of the "Five P" model to assess risk associated with each of the five factors. (FAA-H-8083-2)

At key decision points, application of the Five P checklist should be performed by reviewing each of the critical variables:

Plan—weather, route, publications, ATC reroutes/delays, fuel onboard/remaining

Plane—mechanical status, automation status, database currency, backup systems

Pilot—illness, medication, stress, alcohol, fatigue, eating (I'M SAFE)

Passengers—pilots/non-pilots, nervous or quiet, experienced or new, business or pleasure

Programming—autopilot, GPS, MFD/PFD; anticipate likely reroutes/clearances; questions to ask (What is it doing? Why is it doing it? Did I do it?)

8. When is the use of the "Five P" checklist recommended? (FAA-H-8083-9)

The "Five P" concept relies on the pilot to adopt a scheduled review of the critical variables at points in the flight where decisions are most likely to be effective. These key decision points include preflight, pre-takeoff, hourly or at the midpoint of the flight, pre-descent, and just prior to the final approach fix (or, for VFR operations, just prior to entering the traffic pattern). They also should be used anytime an emergency situation arises.

9. **Describe the 3P model used in ADM.** (FAA-H-8083-2)

The Perceive, Process, Perform (3P) model for ADM offers a simple, practical, and systematic approach that can be used during all phases of flight. To use it, the pilot will:

Perceive the given set of circumstances for a flight; think through circumstances related to the: **P**ilot, **A**ircraft, en**V**ironment, and **E**xternal pressures (**PAVE**). The fundamental question to ask is, "What could hurt me, my passengers, or my aircraft?"

Process by evaluating their impact on flight safety. Think through the **C**onsequences of each hazard, **A**lternatives available, **R**eality of the situation, and **E**xternal pressures (**CARE**) that might influence their analysis.

Perform by implementing the best course of action. **T**ransfer (can the risk decision be transferred to someone else; can you consult someone?); **E**liminate (is there a way to eliminate the hazard?); **A**ccept (do the benefits of accepting risk outweigh the costs?); **M**itigate (what can you do to reduce the risk?) (**TEAM**)

10. **Explain how often a pilot should use the 3P model of ADM throughout a flight.** (FAA-H-8083-9)

Once a pilot has completed the 3P decision process and selected a course of action, the process begins again because the circumstances brought about by the course of action require analysis. The decision-making process is a continuous loop of perceiving, processing and performing.

F. Adverse Weather

1. When attempting to circumnavigate thunderstorms, what minimum distance is recommended? (AIM 7-1-29)

Thunderstorms identified as severe or displaying an intense radar echo should be avoided by at least 20 miles. This is especially true under the anvil of a large cumulonimbus.

2. In the event that you inadvertently enter a thunderstorm, what recommended procedures should you follow? (AIM 7-1-29)

a. Tighten your safety belt, put on your shoulder harness if you have one, and secure all loose objects.

b. Keep your eyes on your instruments. Looking outside the cockpit can increase the danger of temporary blindness from lightning.

c. Plan your course to take you through the storm in a minimum time and hold it. Don't turn back once you are in the thunderstorm. Remember that turning maneuvers increase stresses on the aircraft.

d. To avoid the most critical icing, establish a penetration altitude below the freezing level or above the level of -15°C.

e. Turn on pitot heat and carburetor or jet inlet heat. Icing can be rapid at any altitude and cause almost instantaneous power failure or loss of airspeed indication.

f. Establish power settings for reduced turbulence penetration airspeed recommended in your aircraft manual. Reduced airspeed lessens the structural stresses on the aircraft.

g. Turn up cockpit lights to highest intensity to lessen danger of temporary blindness from lightning.

h. If using automatic pilot, disengage altitude hold mode and speed hold mode. The automatic altitude and speed controls will increase maneuvers of the aircraft, thus increasing structural stresses.

i. Maintain a constant attitude; let the aircraft "ride the waves." Maneuvers to try to maintain constant altitude increase stresses on the aircraft.

3. Describe the hazardous aircraft icing conditions a pilot may encounter in the following cloud types and conditions: stratus, cumulus, freezing rain, and drizzle. (AC 91-74)

Stratus clouds—These form a stratified layer that may cover a wide area; the lifting processes that form them are usually gradual so they rarely have exceptionally high liquid water content. Icing layers in stratus clouds with a vertical thickness in excess of 3,000 feet are rare, so either climbing or descending may be effective in exiting the icing conditions within the clouds.

Cumuliform clouds—Hazardous icing conditions can occur in cumulus clouds, which sometimes have very high liquid water content. It is not advisable to fly through a series of such clouds or to execute holds within them. However, because these clouds normally do not extend very far horizontally, any icing encountered in such a cloud may be of limited duration and it may be possible to deviate around the cloud.

Freezing rain—Freezing rain forms when rain becomes super-cooled by falling through a subfreezing layer of air. It may be possible to exit the freezing rain by climbing into the warm layer.

Freezing drizzle—Because freezing drizzle often forms by the collision-coalescence process, the pilot should not assume that a warm layer of air exists above the aircraft. A pilot encountering freezing drizzle should exit the conditions as quickly as possible either vertically or horizontally. The three possible actions are to ascend to an altitude where the freezing drizzle event is less intense, to descend to an area of warmer air, or to make a level turn to emerge from the area of freezing drizzle.

4. What action is recommended if you inadvertently encounter icing conditions? (FAA-H-8083-15)

You should leave the area of visible moisture. This might mean descending to an altitude below the cloud bases, climbing to an altitude above the cloud tops, or turning to a different course. If this is not possible, then the pilot must move to an altitude where the temperature is above freezing. If you're going to climb, do so quickly; procrastination may leave you with too much ice. If you're going to descend, you must know the temperature of the air and the type of terrain below.

5. If an airplane has anti-icing and/or deicing equipment installed, can it be flown into icing conditions? (FAA-H-8083-3)

The presence of anti-icing and deicing equipment does not necessarily mean that an airplane is approved for flight in icing conditions. The AFM/POH, placards, and manufacturer should be consulted for specific determination of approvals and limitations.

6. A pilot flying an aircraft certificated for flight in known Icing (FIKI) should be aware of a phenomenon known as "roll upset." What is roll upset? (FAA-H-8083-15)

Roll upset is an uncommanded and uncontrolled roll phenomenon associated with severe in-flight icing. It can occur without the usual symptoms of ice accumulation or a perceived aerodynamic stall. Pilots flying certificated FIKI aircraft should be aware that severe icing is a condition outside of the aircraft's certification icing envelope. The roll upset that occurs may be caused by airflow separation (aerodynamic stall), which induces self-deflection of the ailerons and loss of or degraded roll handling characteristics. The aileron deflection may be caused by ice accumulating in a sensitive area of the wing aft of the deicing boots.

7. What is the recommended recovery procedure for a roll upset? (AC 91-51)

a. Reduce the angle of attack by increasing airspeed. If in a turn, roll wings level.

b. Set appropriate power and monitor the airspeed and angle of attack. A controlled descent is a vastly better alternative than an uncontrolled descent.

c. If flaps are extended, do not retract them unless you can determine that the upper surface of the airfoil is clear of ice, because retracting the flaps will increase the AOA at a given airspeed.

d. Verify that wing ice protection is functioning normally by visual observation of the left and right wing.

8. What is a tailplane stall? (AC 91-51; AC 91-74)

A tailplane stall occurs when a tailplane, with accumulated ice, is placed at a sufficiently negative AOA and stalls. Since the tailplane counters the natural nose-down tendency caused by the center of lift of the main wing, the airplane will react by pitching down, sometimes uncontrollably, when the tailplane is stalled.

9. What changes in airplane configuration can aggravate a tailplane stall condition? (AC 91-74)

Most aircraft have a nose-down pitching moment from the wings because the CG is ahead of the CP (center of pressure). The tailplane counteracts this moment by providing a downward force. The result of this configuration is that actions which move the wing away from stall, such as deployment of flaps or increasing speed, may increase the negative AOA of the tail. With ice on the tailplane, it may stall after full or partial deployment of flaps.

10. How can tailplane icing be detected? (AC 91-51)

Any of the following symptoms, occurring individually or in combination, may be a warning of tailplane icing:

a. Elevator control pulsing, oscillations, or vibrations

b. Abnormal nose-down trim change

c. Any other unusual or abnormal pitch anomalies (possibly resulting in pilot induced oscillations)

d. Reduction or loss of elevator effectiveness

e. Sudden change in elevator force (control would move nose-down if unrestrained)

f. Sudden uncommanded nose-down pitch

11. How is recovery from a tailplane stall accomplished? (AC 91-51)

At the slightest indication of a tail stall, the pilot should:

a. Immediately retract the flaps to the previous setting and apply appropriate nose-up elevator pressure.

b. Increase airspeed appropriately for the reduced flap extension setting.

c. Apply sufficient power for aircraft configuration and conditions. (High engine power settings may adversely impact response to tailplane stall conditions at high airspeed in some aircraft designs. Observe the manufacturer's recommendations regarding power settings.)

d. Make nose-down pitch changes slowly, even in gusting conditions, if circumstances allow.

e. If a pneumatic deicing system is used, operate the system several times in an attempt to clear the tailplane of ice.

Remember: Recovery procedures from an ice-induced tailplane stall are opposite from those for an ice-induced wing stall.

12. If icing is inadvertently encountered, how would configuration for approach and landing be different? (AC 91-74)

a. Extension of landing gear may create excessive drag when coupled with ice. Flaps should be deployed in stages, carefully noting the aircraft's behavior at each stage.

b. If anomalies occur, it is best not to increase the amount of flaps and perhaps even to retract them depending on how much the aircraft is deviating from normal performance.

c. If landing with an accumulation of ice, use a higher approach speed.

d. During the landing flare, carry higher-than-normal power if there is ice on the airplane. Use a longer runway if available.

e. After touchdown, use brakes sparingly to prevent skidding. Be prepared for possible loss of directional control caused by ice buildup on landing gear.

G. Navigation Systems

1. Within what frequency range do VORs operate? (AIM 1-1-3)

VORs operate within the 108.0 to 117.95 MHz VHF band.

2. What restrictions are VORs subject to? (AIM 1-1-3)

VORs are subject to line-of-sight restrictions, and the range varies proportionally to the altitude of the receiving equipment.

3. What are the normal usable distances for the various classes of VOR stations? (AIM 1-1-8)

H-VORs and L-VORs have a normal usable distance of 40 nautical miles below 18,000 feet. T-VORs are short range facilities which have a power output of approximately 50 watts and a usable distance of 25 nautical miles at 12,000 feet and below. T-VORs are used primarily for instrument approaches in terminal areas, on or adjacent to airports.

VOR Standard Service Volumes

SSV Class Designator	Altitude and Range Boundaries	
Terminal	1,000 to 12,000 feet AGL	25 NM
Low-altitude	1,000 to 18,000 feet AGL	40 NM
High-altitude	1,000 to 14,500 feet AGL	40 NM
High-altitude	14,500 to 18,000 feet AGL	100 NM
High-altitude	18,000 to 45,000 feet AGL	130 NM
High-altitude	45,000 to 60,000 feet AGL	100 NM

4. What is the meaning of a single coded identification received only once every 30 seconds from a VORTAC station? (AIM 1-1-7 and 1-1-12)

The DME component is operative; the VOR component is inoperative. It is important to recognize which identifier is retained for the operative facility. A single coded identifier with a repeat interval every 30 seconds indicates DME is operative. If no identification is received, the facility has been taken off the air for tune-up or repair, even though intermittent or constant signals are received.

5. Will all VOR stations have the capability of providing distance information to aircraft equipped with DME? (AIM 1-1-7)

No, aircraft receiving equipment ensures reception of azimuth and distance information from a common source only when designated as VOR/DME, VORTAC, ILS/DME, and LOC/DME stations.

6. For IFR operations off established airways, the "Route of Flight" portion of an IFR flight plan should list VOR navigational aids that are no further than what distance from each other? (AIM 5-1-8)

Below 18,000 feet MSL, use aids not more than 80 NM apart.

Between 14,500 feet MSL and 17,999 feet MSL in the conterminous U.S., H (high-altitude service volume) facilities not more than 200 NM apart may be used.

7. What angular deviation from a VOR course is represented by half-scale deflection of the CDI? (FAA-H-8083-15)

Full scale deflection = 10°; therefore, half-scale deflection = 5°.

8. What are the essential components of all VOR indicator instruments? (FAA-H-8083-15)

a. Omnibearing selector (OBS)

b. Course deviation indicator (CDI)

c. TO/FROM indicator

d. Flags or other signal strength indicators

9. What is reverse sensing? (FAA-H-8083-15)

Reverse sensing is when the VOR needle indicates the reverse of normal operation. This occurs when the aircraft is headed toward the station with a FROM indication or when the aircraft is headed away from the station with a TO indication. Also, unless the aircraft has reverse sensing capability and it is in use, when flying inbound on the back course or outbound on the front course of an ILS, reverse sensing will occur.

10. What is the procedure for determining an intercept angle when intercepting a VOR radial? (FAA-H-8083-15)

    a. Turn to a heading to parallel the desired course, in the same direction as the course to be flown.

    b. Determine the difference between the radial to be intercepted and the radial on which you are located.

    c. Double the difference to determine the interception angle, which will not be less than 20° nor greater than 90°.

    d. Rotate the OBS to the desired radial or inbound course.

    e. Turn to the interception heading.

    f. Hold this heading constant until the CDI centers, which indicates the aircraft is on course. (With practice in judging the varying rates of closure with the course centerline, you learn to lead the turn to prevent overshooting the course.)

    g. Turn to the MH corresponding to the selected course and follow tracking procedures inbound or outbound.

Note: Steps a. through c. may be omitted if you turn directly to intercept the course without initially turning to parallel the desired course.

11. What degree of accuracy can be expected in VOR navigation? (AIM 1-1-3)

VOR navigation is accurate to ±1°.

12. Within what frequency range do NDBs normally operate? (AIM 1-1-2)

NDBs operate within the low-to-medium frequency band—190 to 535 kHz.

13. When a radio beacon is used in conjunction with an ILS marker beacon, what is it called? (AIM 1-1-2)

It is called a compass locator.

14. There are four types of NDB facilities in use. What are they and what are their effective ranges? (AIM 1-1-8)

HH facilities: 2,000 watts.................................75 NM
H facilities: 50 to 1,999 watts ....50 NM
MH facilities: less than 50 watts ....25 NM
ILS compass locator: less than 25 watts..........15 NM

15. What limitations apply when using an NDB for navigation? (AIM 1-1-2)

Radio beacons are subject to disturbances that may result in erroneous bearing information. Disturbances result from factors such as lightning, precipitation static, etc. At night, radio beacons are vulnerable to interference from distance stations.

16. What operational procedure should be used when navigation or approaches are conducted using an NDB? (AIM 1-1-2)

Since ADF receivers do not incorporate signal flags to warn a pilot when erroneous bearing information is being displayed, the pilot should continuously monitor the NDB's coded identification.

17. How do you find an ADF relative bearing? (FAA-H-8083-15)

A relative bearing is the angular relationship between the aircraft heading and the station, measured clockwise from the nose. The bearing is read directly on the ADF dial, measured clockwise from zero.

18. How do you find an ADF magnetic bearing? (FAA-H-8083-15)

A magnetic bearing is the direction of an imaginary line from the aircraft to the station or the station to the aircraft referenced to magnetic north. To determine, use this formula:

MH + RB = MB
(Magnetic heading + relative bearing = magnetic bearing)

If the sum is more than 360, subtract 360 to get the magnetic bearing to the station. The reciprocal of this number is the magnetic bearing from the station.

19. What is ADF homing? (FAA-H-8083-15)

ADF homing is flying the aircraft on any heading required to keep the ADF needle on zero until the station is reached.

20. What is ADF tracking? (FAA-H-8083-15)

ADF tracking is a procedure used to fly a straight geographic flight path inbound to or from an NDB. A heading is established that will maintain the desired track, compensating for wind drift.

21. You are tracking inbound to an NDB, your heading equals your course and the ADF needle is now pointing 10° to the left. What procedure will you use for wind drift correction? (FAA-H-8083-15)

Turn 20° left. When the needle is deflected 20° (deflection = interception angle), track has been intercepted. The aircraft is on track as long as the RB remains the same number of degrees as the wind correction angle (WCA). Lead the interception to avoid overshooting the track. Turn 10° toward the inbound course. You are now inbound with a 10° left correction angle.

22. What is an HSI? (FAA-H-8083-15)

The horizontal situation indicator (HSI) is a direction indicator that uses the output from a flux valve to drive the compass card. The HSI combines the magnetic compass with navigation signals/ glideslope and gives the pilot an indication of the location of the aircraft with relationship to the chosen course or radial. The aircraft magnetic heading is displayed on the compass card under the lubber line and the course select pointer shows the course selected and its reciprocal. The course deviation bar operates with a VOR/ Localizer (VOR/LOC) or GPS navigation receiver to indicate left or right deviations from the course selected with the course select pointer. The desired course is selected by rotating the course select pointer in relation to the compass card by means of the course select knob. The HSI has a fixed aircraft symbol and the course deviation bar displays the aircraft's position relative to the selected course.

23. What is DME? (AIM 1-1-7)

DME stands for distance measuring equipment. Aircraft equipped with DME are provided with distance and ground speed information when receiving a VORTAC or TACAN facility. In the operation of DME, paired pulses at a specific spacing are sent out from the aircraft and are received at the ground station. The ground station then transmits paired pulses back to the aircraft at the same pulse spacing but on a different frequency. The time required for the round trip of this signal exchange is measured in the airborne DME unit and is translated into distance and ground speed. Reliable signals may be received at distances up to 199 NM at line-of-sight altitude. DME operates on frequencies in the UHF spectrum from 960 MHz to 1215 MHz. Distance information is slant-range distance, not horizontal.

24. When is DME equipment required? (14 CFR 91.205)

If VOR navigational equipment is required for flight at and above FL240, the aircraft must be equipped with approved DME or a suitable RNAV system. If the DME or RNAV system fails at or above FL240, the pilot-in-command shall notify ATC immediately, and then may continue operations to the next airport of intended landing where repairs or equipment replacement can be done.

25. As a rule-of-thumb, to minimize DME slant-range error, how far from the facility should you be to consider the reading accurate? (FAA-H-8083-15)

Slant-range error will be at a minimum if the aircraft is one or more miles from the facility for each 1,000 feet of altitude above the facility.

26. What is RNAV? (P/CG)

Area navigation (RNAV) is a method of navigation that permits aircraft operation on any desired flight path within the coverage of ground- or space-based navigation aids or within the limits of the capability of self-contained aids, or a combination of these.

27. Give a brief description of the Global Positioning System. (AIM 1-1-18)

GPS is a satellite-based radio navigation system that broadcasts a signal used by receivers to determine precise position anywhere in the world. The receiver tracks multiple satellites and determines a pseudo-range measurement that is then used to determine user location.

28. How many satellites does a GPS receiver require to compute its position? (AIM 1-1-18)

The GPS constellation of 24 satellites is designed so that a minimum of five is always observable by a user anywhere on earth. The receiver uses data from a minimum of four satellites above the mask angle (the lowest angle above the horizon at which it can use a satellite).

3 satellites—yields a latitude and longitude position only (2D)
4 satellites—yields latitude, longitude, and altitude position (3D)
5 satellites—3D and RAIM
6 satellites—3D and RAIM isolates corrupt signal and removes from navigation solution

29. What are the various Technical Standard Orders that apply to GPS navigation equipment? (AC 90-100)

TSO-C129—Airborne Supplemental Navigation Equipment Using the GPS (non-WAAS)

TSO-C196—Airborne Supplemental Navigation Sensors for GPS Equipment Using Aircraft-Based Augmentation (non-WAAS)

TSO-C145—Airborne Navigation Sensors Using the GPS Augmented by WAAS

TSO-C146—Stand-Alone Airborne Navigation Equipment Using the GPS Augmented by WAAS

30. What is "WAAS"? (FAA-H-8261-1)

The Wide Area Augmentation System, as its name implies, augments the basic GPS satellite constellation with additional ground stations and enhanced position integrity information transmitted from geostationary satellites. This capability of augmentation enhances both the accuracy and integrity of basic GPS, and may support electronic vertical guidance approach minimums as low as 200 feet HAT and ½ SM visibility.

31. Briefly describe the operation of WAAS. (FAA-H-8083-30)

WAAS ground stations receive GPS signals and forward position errors to two master ground stations. Time and location information is analyzed, and correction instructions are sent to communication satellites in geostationary orbit over the National Airspace System (NAS). The satellites broadcast GPS-like signals that WAAS-enabled GPS receivers use to correct position information received from GPS satellites. A WAAS-enabled GPS receiver (TSO-C145A or TSO-146A) is required to use the wide area augmentation system.

32. In what ways can RNAV equipment be used as a substitute means of navigation guidance? (AIM 1-2-3)

Suitable RNAV Systems (TSO-C129/-C196/-C145/-C146) may be used in the following ways:

a. To determine aircraft position relative to, or distance from, a VOR, TACAN, NDB, compass locator, DME fix; or a named fix defined by a VOR radial, TACAN course, NDB bearing, or compass locator bearing intersecting a VOR or localizer course.

b. Navigate to or from a VOR, TACAN, NDB, or compass locator.

c. Hold over a VOR, TACAN, NDB, compass locator, or DME fix.

d. Fly an arc based upon DME.

Note: These operations are allowable even when a facility is identified as required on a procedure (for example, "Note ADF required").

33. **What are several examples of operations where RNAV equipment cannot be used as a substitute means of navigation?** (AIM 1-2-3)

    a. Lateral navigation on localizer-based courses (including localizer back-course guidance) without reference to raw localizer data.

    b. Procedures that are identified as not authorized ("NA") by NOTAM, without exception.

    c. Pilots may not substitute for the NAVAID (for example, a VOR or NDB) providing lateral guidance for the final approach segment. This restriction does not refer to instrument approach procedures with "or GPS" in the title when using GPS or WAAS.

34. **When using RNAV equipment for navigation, what is the difference between the terms "Track (TRK)" and "Desired Track (DTK)?"** (FAA-H-8083-6; P/CG)

    Track—the actual flight path of an aircraft over the surface of the earth. The track, which is the result of aircraft heading and winds, tells you which direction the aircraft is actually flying. Winds make it likely that the track and heading will be different.

    Desired Track—the planned or intended track between two waypoints. Desired track is measured in degrees from either magnetic or true north. The instantaneous angle may change from point to point along the great circle track between waypoints. The desired track is the intended course for the active leg in the programmed flight plan.

35. **Why is there a difference between the distance information provided by a GPS receiver and the distance information provided by conventional DME equipment?** (AIM 1-1-18)

    Variations in distances will occur since GPS distance-to-waypoint values are along-track distances (ATD) computed to the next waypoint, and the DME values published on underlying procedures are slant-range distances measured to the station. This difference increases with aircraft altitude and proximity to the NAVAID.

36. **When navigating with GPS equipment, explain the CDI scaling changes (sensitivity) that occur for the appropriate route segment and phase of flight.** (AIM 1-1-18)

Departures and DPs (Terminal mode)	CDI sensitivity = ±1 NM
More than 30 NM from the destination	CDI sensitivity = ±5 NM (±2 NM WAAS)
Within 30 NM from destination (Terminal mode)	CDI sensitivity = ±1 NM
Within 2 NM from FAWP (Approach mode armed)	CDI sensitivity = ±1 NM to ±0.3 NM at the FAWP
Missed approach segment	CDI sensitivity = ±0.3 NM to ±1 NM

Note: Be familiar with the distance and approach parameters that change the CDI scaling for your aircraft's class of equipment.

37. **What is OBS or non-sequencing mode?** (FAA-H-8083-6)

OBS or non-sequencing mode is a FMS/RNAV navigation mode that does not automatically sequence between waypoints in the programmed route. The non-sequencing mode maintains the current active waypoint indefinitely, and allows the pilot to specify desired track to or from that waypoint.

38. **What is the purpose of baro-aiding?** (AIM 1-1-18)

Baro-aiding is a method of augmenting the GPS integrity solution by using a non-satellite input source (aircraft static system) to provide a vertical reference. GPS derived altitude should not be relied upon to determine aircraft altitude since the vertical error can be quite large and no integrity is provided. To ensure that baro-aiding is available, the current altimeter setting must be entered into the receiver. Baro-aiding satisfies the RAIM requirement in lieu of a fifth satellite.

39. What is "required navigation performance" (RNP)? (AIM 1-2-2)

RNP is RNAV with on-board navigation monitoring and alerting. RNP is also a statement of navigation performance necessary for operation within a defined airspace. A critical component of RNP is the ability of the aircraft navigation system to monitor its achieved navigation performance, and to identify for the pilot whether the operational requirement is or is not being met during an operation. RNP-0.3 will be used for approaches, and refers to 0.3 nautical mile accuracy, which may be achieved through various means (GPS, WAAS, FMS with DME updates), but your aircraft will be certified to a particular RNP. The FAA is moving toward a performance-based national airspace system.

40. What is ADS-B? (P/CG)

Automatic dependent surveillance–broadcast (ADS-B) is a surveillance system in which an aircraft to be detected is fitted with cooperative equipment in the form of a data link transmitter. The aircraft broadcasts its GPS-derived position and other information such as position, altitude, and velocity over the data link, which is received by a ground-based transmitter/receiver (transceiver) for processing and display at an ATC facility. In addition, aircraft equipped with ADS-B IN capability can also receive these broadcasts and display the information to improve the pilot's situational awareness of other traffic. ADS-B is automatic because no external interrogation is required. It is dependent because it relies on onboard position sources and broadcast transmission systems to provide surveillance information to ATC, and other users.

H. Airway Route System

1. What are the designated altitudes for the airways in the VOR and L/MF Airway System? (AIM 5-3-4)

The VOR and L/MF Airway System consists of airways designated from 1,200 feet above the surface (or in some instances higher) up to but not including 18,000 feet MSL. These airways are depicted on Enroute Low Altitude Charts.

2. What are the lateral limits of low altitude federal airways? (FAA-H-8083-15)

Each federal airway includes the airspace within parallel boundary lines 4 NM each side of the centerline.

3. How are airways and route systems depicted on enroute low altitude charts? (AIM 5-3-4)

VHF/UHF data is depicted in black. LF/MF data is depicted in brown. RNAV route data is depicted in blue.

Note: Segments of VOR airways in Alaska are based on L/MF navigation aids and charted in brown instead of black on en route charts.

4. What is a "changeover point"? (AIM 5-3-6)

It is a point along the route or airway segment between two adjacent navigational facilities or waypoints where changeover in navigational guidance should occur.

5. What is a mileage breakdown point? (FAA-H-8083-15)

Occasionally an "x" will appear at a separated segment of an airway that is not an intersection. The "x" is a mileage breakdown or computer navigation fix and indicates a course change.

6. What is a "waypoint"? (P/CG)

It is a predetermined geographical position used for route/instrument approach definition, progress reports, published VFR routes, visual reporting points or points for transitioning and/or circumnavigating controlled and/or special use airspace. A waypoint is defined relative to a VORTAC station or in terms of latitude/longitude coordinates.

7. **What is Tower Enroute Control Service?** (FAA-H-8083-15)

At many locations, instrument flights can be conducted entirely in terminal airspace. These tower en route control (TEC) routes are generally for aircraft operating below 10,000 feet, and they can be found in the *Aircraft/Facility Directory*. Pilots desiring to use TEC should include that designation in the remarks section of the flight plan.

8. **Are the courses depicted on an Enroute Low Altitude Chart magnetic or true courses?** (FAA-H-8083-15)

They are magnetic courses.

9. **Describe the climb procedure when approaching a fix beyond which a higher MEA exists.** (14 CFR 91.177)

A pilot may climb to a higher minimum IFR altitude immediately after passing the point beyond which that minimum altitude applies.

10. **Describe the climb procedure when approaching a fix at which a MCA exists.** (FAA-H-8083-15)

A pilot should initiate a climb so the MCA is reached by the time the intersection is crossed. An MCA will be charted when a higher MEA route segment is approached. The MCA is usually indicated when you are approaching steeply rising terrain, and obstacle clearance and/or signal reception is compromised.

11. **What requirement must be met before ATC will allow an aircraft to operate on an unpublished RNAV route?** (AIM 5-3-4)

Unpublished RNAV routes are direct routes, based on area navigation capability between waypoints defined in terms of latitude/longitude coordinates, degree-distance fixes, or offsets from established routes/airways at a specified distance and direction. Radar monitoring by ATC is required on all unpublished RNAV routes.

12. What are "T" and "Q" routes? (AIM 5-3-4)

Published RNAV routes that can be flight-planned for use by aircraft with RNAV capability. They are depicted in blue on aeronautical charts and are identified by the letter T or Q, followed by the airway number (e.g., T-205, Q-13). They provide more direct routing for IFR aircraft and enhance system safety and efficiency.

T-routes—depicted on Enroute Low Altitude Charts; available for use by RNAV equipped aircraft from 1,200 feet above the surface (or in some instances higher) up to but not including 18,000 feet MSL.

Q-routes—depicted on Enroute High Altitude Charts; available for use by RNAV equipped aircraft between 18,000 feet MSL and FL450 inclusive.

13. For the following terms, identify the symbols which correspond to them on Enroute Low Altitude Charts.

(These symbols might not all be on your Enroute Low Altitude Chart.)

VOR /DME	
TACAN	
VOR	
VORTAC	
RNAV waypoint compulsory position point	NAMEE N00°00.00' W00°00.00'
RNAV waypoint noncompulsory position point	NAMEE N00°00.00' W00°00.00'
NDB	(Brown) (Blue) (Brown, blue box)
Commercial broadcast station	WKBW 1520

Compass locator frequency	**NAME** NAM ⸗⸗⸗ _000_ DME Chan 00
Localizer facility information box	**NAME** NAM ⸗⸗⸗ 000.0(T) DME Chan 00 MN ⸗⸗ 000
VORTAC facility information box	LEXINGTON 112.6 HYK 73 ⸗⸗⸗ - N37°57.98' W84°28.35' ⌐ LOUISVILLE ⌐
Controlling FSS	123.6 122.6 122.1 R 122.1 R **FAYETTEVILLE FYV** WASHINGTON
Remote air/ground communications with ARTCC	NAME Name 134.3 269.5
Airport with a published instrument approach	**AIRPORT DATA** Airports/Seaplane bases shown in BLUE and GREEN have an approved Low Altitude Instrument Approach Procedure published. Those in BLUE have an approved DOD Low Altitude Instrument Approach Procedure and/or DOD RADAR MINIMA published in DOD FLIPS or Alaska Terminal. Airports/Seaplane bases shown in BROWN do not have a published Instrument Approach Procedure.
Airport without a published instrument approach	*(see above)*
Compass rose	
ATC compulsory reporting point	▲ ▲ **ALANA** **ATTIC**
ATC noncompulsory reporting point	**ALANA** **ATTIC** △ △
DME fix distance when not obvious	⑮ →
DME fix distance when the same as route miles	→
VOR changeover point	42 ⌐⌐ 26

Mileage break at an airway course change, intersection, or breakdown point	32 △/x 25
Mileage between VORs or a VOR and compulsory reporting point	123 (123)
Mileage Breakdown or Computer Navigation Fix	X X
CNF with no ATC Function	(RCRCP)
Victor airway	V10
ARTCC boundary, controlling ARTCC	NEW YORK WASHINGTON
MOCA All altitudes are MSL unless otherwise noted.	LOW ALTITUDE 5500 *3500 ← MOCA → 5500 *3500 V4 AO 7000G *6300 T266 112
MEA All altitudes are MSL unless otherwise noted.	LOW ALTITUDE 3500 30000G RNAV/GPS MEA 3500 V4 AO 5500→ ←3500 Directional MEA 5500 → ←3500 V4 AO
Off Route Obstruction Clearance Altitude (OROCA)	LOW ALTITUDE 12^5 Example: 12,500 feet
Change in MEA or MOCA at other than NAVAIDs	⊣ ⊢
Minimum Crossing Altitude	MCA V6 4000S /X/
Minimum Reception Altitude	MRA 9000 /R/

Maximum Authorized Altitude	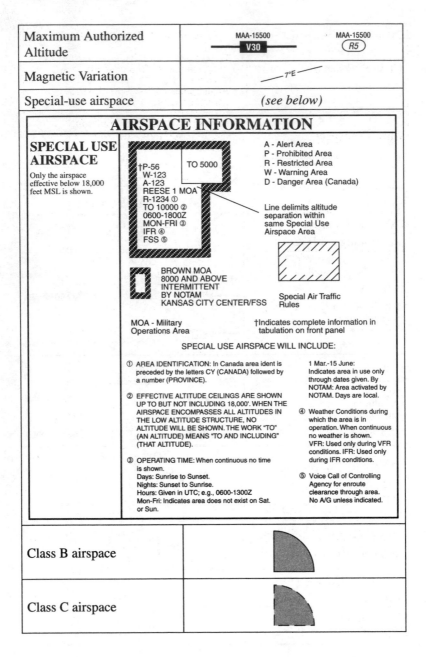
Magnetic Variation	
Special-use airspace	*(see below)*

AIRSPACE INFORMATION

SPECIAL USE AIRSPACE

Only the airspace effective below 18,000 feet MSL is shown.

†P-56
W-123
A-123
REESE 1 MOA
R-1234 ①
TO 10000 ②
0600-1800Z
MON-FRI ③
IFR ④
FSS ⑤

TO 5000

A - Alert Area
P - Prohibited Area
R - Restricted Area
W - Warning Area
D - Danger Area (Canada)

Line delimits altitude separation within same Special Use Airspace Area

BROWN MOA
8000 AND ABOVE
INTERMITTENT
BY NOTAM
KANSAS CITY CENTER/FSS

Special Air Traffic Rules

MOA - Military Operations Area

†Indicates complete information in tabulation on front panel

SPECIAL USE AIRSPACE WILL INCLUDE:

① AREA IDENTIFICATION: In Canada area ident is preceded by the letters CY (CANADA) followed by a number (PROVINCE).

② EFFECTIVE ALTITUDE CEILINGS ARE SHOWN UP TO BUT NOT INCLUDING 18,000'. WHEN THE AIRSPACE ENCOMPASSES ALL ALTITUDES IN THE LOW ALTITUDE STRUCTURE, NO ALTITUDE WILL BE SHOWN. THE WORK "TO" (AN ALTITUDE) MEANS "TO AND INCLUDING" (THAT ALTITUDE).

③ OPERATING TIME: When continuous no time is shown.
Days: Sunrise to Sunset.
Nights: Sunset to Sunrise.
Hours: Given in UTC; e.g., 0600-1300Z
Mon-Fri: Indicates area does not exist on Sat. or Sun.

1 Mar.-15 June:
Indicates area in use only through dates given. By NOTAM: Area activated by NOTAM. Days are local.

④ Weather Conditions during which the area is in operation. When continuous no weather is shown.
VFR: Used only during VFR conditions. IFR: Used only during IFR conditions.

⑤ Voice Call of Controlling Agency for enroute clearance through area. No A/G unless indicated.

Class B airspace	
Class C airspace	

	AIRSPACE INFORMATION
Class E airspace	Open area (white) indicates controlled airspace (Class E) unless otherwise indicated. All airspace 14,500' and above is controlled (Class E).
Class G airspace	Shaded area (brown) indicates uncontrolled airspace below 14,500' (Class G).
Mode C area	MODE C 30 NM (a solid blue outline)
ARTCC boundaries	⊓⊔⊓⊔⊓⊔⊓⊔
ARTCC Remoted VHF/ UHF frequency site	NAME Name 000.0 000.0
Air Defense Identification Zone (ADIZ)	⁚⁚⁚⁚⁚⁚⁚⁚⁚⁚⁚⁚⁚⁚⁚
ASOS/AWOS	Ⓐ
HIWAS	Ⓗ
TWEB	Ⓣ
ILS localizer course with ATC function	
ATIS	(Airport Name)Ⓓ 280 Ⓛ* 43s Automatic Terminal ⟶ (A) *109.8 Information Service
Pilot Controlled Lighting	Ⓛ
Special VFR not authorized	No SVFR

I. Airspace

1. What is Class A airspace? (AIM 3-2-2)

Generally, that airspace from 18,000 feet MSL up to and including FL600, including airspace overlying the waters within 12 nautical miles off the coast of the 48 contiguous states and Alaska; and designated international airspace beyond 12 nautical miles off the coast of the 48 contiguous states and Alaska within areas of domestic radio navigational signal or ATC radar coverage, and within which domestic procedures are applied.

2. What is Class B airspace? (AIM 3-2-3)

Generally, that airspace from the surface to 10,000 feet MSL surrounding the nation's busiest airports in terms of IFR operations or passenger enplanements. The configuration of each Class B airspace area is individually tailored and consists of a surface area and two or more layers (some resemble an upside-down wedding cake), and is designated to contain all published instrument procedures once an aircraft enters the airspace. An ATC clearance is required for all aircraft to operate in the area, and all aircraft cleared as such receive separation services within the airspace. The visibility and cloud clearance requirement for VFR operations is 3 statute miles visibility and clear of clouds.

3. What is Class C airspace? (AIM 3-2-4)

Generally, that airspace from the surface to 4,000 feet above the airport elevation (charted in MSL) surrounding airports that have an operational control tower, are serviced by a radar approach control, and that have a certain number of IFR operations or passenger enplanements. Although the configuration of each Class C airspace area is individually tailored, the airspace usually consists of a 5 NM radius core surface area that extends from the surface up to 4,000 feet above the airport elevation, and a 10 NM radius shelf area that extends from 1,200 feet to 4,000 feet above the airport elevation.

4. What is Class D airspace? (AIM 3-2-5)

Generally, that airspace from the surface to 2,500 feet above the airport elevation (charted in MSL) surrounding airports that have an operational control tower. The configuration of each Class D airspace area is individually tailored, and when instrument procedures are published, the airspace will usually be designed to contain those procedures.

5. When a control tower, located at an airport within Class D airspace, ceases operation for the day, what happens to the lower limit of the controlled airspace? (AIM 3-2-5)

During the hours the tower is not in operation, Class E surface area rules, or a combination of Class E rules to 700 feet AGL and Class G rules to the surface, will become applicable. Check the A/FD for specifics.

6. What is Class E (controlled) airspace? (AIM 3-2-6)

Generally, if the airspace is not Class A, Class B, Class C, or Class D, and it is controlled airspace, it is Class E airspace. Class E airspace extends upward from either the surface or a designated altitude to the overlying controlled airspace. When designated as a surface area, the airspace will be configured to contain all instrument procedures. Also in this class are federal airways, airspace beginning at either 700 or 1,200 feet AGL used to transition to or from the terminal or enroute environment, enroute domestic, and offshore airspace areas designated below 18,000 feet MSL. Unless designated at a lower altitude, Class E airspace begins at 14,500 feet MSL over the United States, including that airspace overlying the waters within 12 nautical miles of the coast of the 48 contiguous states and Alaska, up to, but not including 18,000 feet MSL, and the airspace above FL600.

7. What is the floor of Class E airspace when designated in conjunction with an airport with an approved IAP? (14 CFR 71.71)

700 feet AGL.

8. **What is the floor of Class E airspace when designated in conjunction with a federal airway?** (14 CFR 71.71)

   1,200 feet AGL.

9. **Class E airspace within the contiguous United States extends upward from either 700 feet AGL or 1,200 feet AGL, up to but not including what altitude?** (AIM 3-2-6)

   Except for 18,000 feet MSL, Class E airspace has no defined vertical limit; rather, it extends upward from either the surface or a designated altitude to the overlying or adjacent controlled airspace. Unless designated at a lower altitude, Class E airspace begins at 14,500 feet MSL and extends up to, but not including 18,000 feet MSL, overlying the 48 contiguous states including the waters within 12 miles from the coast of the contiguous states.

10. **What is Class G airspace?** (AIM 3-3-1)

    Class G airspace is that portion of the airspace that has not been designated as Class A, B, C, D, and E airspace.

11. **What are the vertical limits of Class G airspace?**

    Class G airspace begins at the surface and continues up to but not including the overlying controlled airspace, or 14,500 MSL, or where Class E airspace begins, whichever occurs first.

J. Special Use Airspace

1. **Define the following types of airspace.** (AIM 3-4-2 through 3-4-8, and 3-5-3; 14 CFR Part 93)

   Prohibited Area—For security or other reasons, aircraft flight is prohibited.

   Restricted Area—Contains unusual, often invisible hazards to aircraft, flights must have permission from the controlling agency, if VFR. IFR flights will be cleared through or vectored around it.

   Military Operations Area—MOAs consist of airspace of defined vertical and lateral limits established for the purpose of separating certain military training activities from IFR traffic. Permission is not required for VFR flights, but extreme caution should be exercised. IFR flights will be cleared through or vectored around it.

Warning Area—Airspace of defined dimensions extending from 3 nautical miles outward from the coast of the U.S. containing activity that may be hazardous to nonparticipating aircraft. A warning area may be located over domestic or international waters or both. Permission is not required but a flight plan is advised.

Alert Area—Depicted on aeronautical charts to inform nonparticipating pilots of areas that may contain a high volume of pilot training or an unusual type of aerial activity. No permission is required, but VFR flights should exercise extreme caution. IFR flights will be cleared through or vectored around it.

Controlled Firing Areas—CFAs contain activities which, if not conducted in a controlled environment, could be hazardous to nonparticipating aircraft. These activities are suspended immediately when spotter aircraft, radar or ground lookout positions, indicate an aircraft might be approaching the area. CFAs are not charted.

National Security Area—Airspace of defined vertical and lateral dimensions established at locations where there is a requirement for increased security and safety of ground facilities. Pilots are requested to voluntarily avoid flying through the depicted NSA. When it is necessary to provide a greater level of security and safety, flight in NSAs may be temporarily prohibited by regulation under the provisions of 14 CFR §99.7.

Temporary Flight Restrictions—A TFR is a regulatory action issued via the U.S. NOTAM system to restrict certain aircraft from operating within a defined area, on a temporary basis, to protect persons or property in the air or on the ground. They may be issued due to a hazardous condition, a special event, or as a general warning for the entire FAA airspace. TFR information can be obtained from a FSS or on the internet at www.faa.gov.

Special Flight Rules Area—an area of airspace within which Special Federal Aviation Regulations (SFARs) apply. Examples include the Washington, D.C. SFRA and the Grand Canyon SFRA. Established operating requirements and procedures to operate within the SFRA can be found in 14 CFR Part 93 and on the specific chart legend for that area.

2. **Where can information on special use airspace be found?** (AIM 3-4-1)

   Special use airspace (except CFAs) is charted on IFR or visual charts and includes the hours of operation, altitudes, and the controlling agency. Current and scheduled status information on special use airspace can be found on the FAA's SUA website at sua.faa.gov

Additional Study Questions

1. **When reaching a holding fix or point to which cleared, what information will ATC expect you to provide without request?** (AIM 5-3-3)

2. **Why are changeover points established?** (AIM 5-3-6)

3. **What is the purpose of magnetic reference bearings found on IFR Enroute Low/High Altitude charts?** (AIM 5-3-4)

4. **When may a pilot operate an aircraft below the published MEA?** (14 CFR 91.177)

5. **What procedures should be used when flying a DME arc?** (FAA-H-8083-15)

6. **ATC will issue speed adjustments to pilots of radar controlled aircraft. Pilots complying with speed adjustments are expected to maintain airspeed within what tolerances?** (AIM 4-4-12)

7. **Both communication receivers have failed. In what other way could you receive ATC instructions with cell phone or handheld radio unavailable?** (FAA-H-8083-15)

8. **While enroute, operating in IMC, what procedure would you use if all communication and navigation equipment failed (complete system failure)?** (FAA-H-8083-15)

Arrival

A. Approach Control

1. What is a STAR? (AIM 5-4-1)

A Standard Terminal Arrival Route (STAR) is an ATC-coded IFR arrival route established for use by arriving IFR aircraft destined for certain airports. Its purpose is to simplify clearance delivery procedures and facilitate transition between enroute and instrument approach procedures. Reference the Terminal Procedures Publication (TPP) for the availability of STARs.

2. If ATC issues your flight a STAR, must you accept it? (AIM 5-4-1)

You are not required to accept a STAR, but if you do, you must be in possession of at least the approved chart. RNAV STARs must be retrievable by the procedure name from the aircraft database and conform to the charted procedure. Pilots should notify ATC if they do not wish to use a STAR by placing "NO STAR" in the remarks section of the flight plan, or by the less desirable method of verbally stating the same to ATC.

3. What is an RNAV STAR? (FAA-H-8261-1)

STARs designated RNAV serve the same purpose as conventional STARs, but are only used by aircraft equipped with FMS or GPS. An RNAV STAR or STAR transition typically includes flyby waypoints, with fly-over waypoints used only when operationally required. These waypoints may be assigned crossing altitudes and speeds to optimize the descent and deceleration profiles.

4. What does the notation "RNAV1" on an RNAV STAR indicate? (AIM 5-4-1; AC 90-100)

RNAV 1 terminal procedures require that the aircraft's track keeping accuracy remain bound by +1 nautical mile (NM) for 95 percent of the total flight time. All pilots are expected to maintain route centerlines, as depicted by onboard lateral deviation indicators and/or flight guidance during all RNAV operations unless authorized to deviate by ATC or under emergency conditions. All public RNAV STARs are RNAV 1.

5. **What does the clearance "descend via" authorize you to do when navigating on a STAR or RNAV STAR procedure?** (AIM 5-4-1)

Clearance to "descend via" authorizes pilots to:

a. Vertically and laterally navigate on a STAR, RNAV STAR, or flight management system procedure (FMSP).

b. When cleared to a waypoint depicted on a STAR/RNAV STAR/FMSP, descend from a previously assigned altitude at pilot's discretion to the altitude depicted for that waypoint, and once established on the depicted arrival, to navigate laterally and vertically to meet all published restrictions.

6. **What is a terminal arrival area (TAA)?** (FAA-H-8083-6)

A terminal arrival area is a published or assigned track by which aircraft are transitioned from the en route structure to the terminal area. A terminal arrival area consists of a designated volume of airspace designed to allow aircraft to enter a protected area with obstacle clearance and signal reception guaranteed where the initial approach course is intercepted.

7. **How can a pilot determine which area of a TAA the aircraft will enter?** (AIM 1-1-18)

The pilot can determine which area of the TAA they will enter by selecting the IF (IAF) to determine the magnetic bearing TO the center IF (IAF). That bearing should then be compared with the published bearings that define the lateral boundaries of the TAA areas.

8. **Will all RNAV (GPS) approaches have a TAA?** (AIM 5-4-5)

No; The TAA will not be found on all RNAV procedures, particularly in areas of heavy concentration of air traffic. When the TAA is published, it replaces the MSA for that approach procedure.

9. **How are fly-over and fly-by waypoints used in a GPS approach procedure?** (AIM 1-1-18)

Fly-by waypoints are used when an aircraft should begin a turn to the next course prior to reaching the waypoint separating the two route segments. This is known as turn anticipation and is compensated for in the airspace and terrain clearances. Approach waypoints, except for the MAWP and the missed approach holding waypoint (MAHWP), are normally fly-by waypoints.

Fly-over waypoints are used when the aircraft must fly over the point prior to starting a turn. New approach charts depict fly-over waypoints as a circled waypoint symbol. Overlay approach charts and some early stand-alone GPS approach charts may not reflect this convention.

10. **When being radar-vectored for an approach, at what point may you start a descent from your last assigned altitude to a lower altitude if "cleared for the approach"?** (AIM 5-5-4)

Upon receipt of an approach clearance while on an unpublished route or being radar vectored, a pilot will comply with the minimum altitude for IFR and maintain the last assigned altitude until established on a segment of a published route or IAP, at which time published altitudes apply.

11. Define the terms:

Initial approach segment
Intermediate approach segment
Final approach segment
Missed approach segment
(Pilot/Controller Glossary)

An instrument approach procedure may have as many as four separate segments depending upon how the approach procedure is structured.

The *initial approach segment* is that segment between the initial approach fix and the intermediate fix, or the point where the aircraft is established on the intermediate course or final approach course.

The *intermediate approach segment* is between the intermediate fix or point and the final approach fix.

The *final approach segment* is between the final approach fix or point and the runway, airport, or missed approach point.

The *missed approach segment* is between the missed approach point or the point of arrival at decision height, and the missed approach fix at the prescribed altitude.

12. What are standard IFR separation minimums?
(AIM 4-4-11)

When radar is employed in the separation of aircraft at the same altitude, a minimum of 3 miles separation is provided between aircraft operating within 40 miles of the radar antenna site, and 5 miles between aircraft operating beyond 40 miles from the antenna site. These minima may be increased or decreased in certain specific situations.

13. What is a Minimum Vectoring Altitude (MVA)?
(P/CG and AIM 5-4-5)

MVA is the lowest MSL altitude at which an IFR aircraft will be vectored by a radar controller, except as otherwise authorized for radar approaches, departures, and missed approaches. The altitude meets IFR obstacle clearance criteria. It may be lower than the published MEA along an airway or J-route segment. It may be used for radar vectoring only upon the controller's determination that an adequate radar return is being received from the aircraft being controlled. Charts depicting minimum vectoring altitudes are normally available only to the controllers and not to the pilots.

14. What are feeder routes? (FAA-H-8261-1)

A feeder route is a route depicted on IAP charts to designate courses for aircraft to proceed from the enroute structure to the IAF. When a feeder route is designated, the chart provides the course or bearing to be flown, the distance, and the minimum altitude. Enroute airway obstacle clearance criteria apply to feeder routes, providing 1,000 feet of obstacle clearance (2,000 feet in mountainous areas).

15. What procedure is to be used when the clearance "cleared for the visual" is issued? (AIM 5-4-23)

A visual approach is conducted on an IFR flight plan and authorizes a pilot to proceed visually and clear of clouds to the airport. The pilot must have either the airport or the preceding identified aircraft in sight. This approach must be authorized and controlled by the appropriate air traffic control facility. Reported weather at the airport must have a ceiling at or above 1,000 feet and visibility 3 miles or greater.

Visual approaches are an IFR procedure conducted under IFR in visual meteorological conditions. Cloud clearance requirements of 14 CFR §91.155 are not applicable.

16. Describe the term "contact approach." (P/CG)

An approach in which an aircraft on an IFR flight plan, having an air traffic control authorization, operating clear of clouds with at least 1 mile flight visibility and a reasonable expectation of continuing to the destination airport in those conditions, may deviate from the instrument approach procedure and proceed to the destination airport by visual reference to the surface. This approach will only be authorized when requested by the pilot and the reported ground visibility at the destination airport is at least 1 statute mile.

17. When is a procedure turn not required?
(AIM 5-4-9; 14 CFR 91.175)

A procedure turn is not required when:

a. The symbol "No PT" is depicted on the initial segment being used.

b. A RADAR VECTOR to the final approach course is provided.

c. Conducting a timed approach from a holding fix.

d. ATC specifies in the approach clearance "CLEARED STRAIGHT-IN (type) APPROACH."

e. A teardrop procedure turn is depicted and a course reversal is required; this type turn must be executed.

f. A holding pattern replaces a procedure turn; the holding pattern must be followed, except when RADAR VECTORING is provided or when NoPT is shown on the approach course.

g. A procedure turn barb is absent in the plan view; the procedure turn is not authorized.

Note: If a pilot is uncertain whether the ATC clearance intends for a procedure turn to be conducted or to allow for a straight-in approach, the pilot must immediately request clarification from ATC (14 CFR §91.123).

18. What are standard procedure turn limitations?
(AIM 5-4-9)

a. Turn on the depicted side.

b. Adhere to depicted minimum altitudes.

c. Complete the maneuver within the distance specified in the profile view.

d. Maneuver at a maximum speed not greater than 200 knots (IAS).

19. What procedure is followed when a holding pattern is specified in lieu of a procedure turn? (AIM 5-4-9)

A holding pattern, in lieu of a procedure turn, may be specified for course reversal in some procedures: the holding pattern is established over an intermediate fix or final approach fix. The holding pattern distance or time specified in the profile view must be observed. Maximum holding airspeed limitations apply, as set forth for all holding patterns. The holding pattern maneuver is completed when the aircraft is established on the inbound course after executing the appropriate entry. If cleared for the approach prior to returning to the holding fix, and the aircraft is at the prescribed altitude, additional circuits of the holding pattern are not necessary nor expected by ATC. If pilots elect to make additional circuits to lose altitude or to become better established on course, it is their responsibility to so advise ATC upon receipt of their approach clearance.

B. Precision Approaches

1. What is a precision approach (PA)? (AIM 5-4-5)

A precision approach (PA) is an instrument approach that is based on a navigation system that provides course and glidepath deviation information meeting the precision standards of ICAO Annex 10. For example, PAR, ILS, and GLS are precision approaches.

2. What are the basic components of a standard ILS? (AIM 1-1-9)

Guidance information...................... localizer, glide slope

Range information ...., marker beacons, DME

Visual information.......................... approach lights, touchdown and centerline lights, runway lights

3. **Describe both visual and aural indications that a pilot would receive when crossing the outer, middle, and inner markers of a standard ILS.** (AIM 1-1-9)

Outer Marker	Middle Marker	Inner Marker
blue light	amber light	white light
dull tone	medium tone	high tone
slow speed	medium speed	high speed
— — — — —	— . — . — .	. . . . . .

4. **What are the distances from the landing threshold of the outer, middle, and inner markers?** (AIM 1-1-9)

Outer marker...................... 4 to 7 miles from threshold

Middle marker .... 3,500 feet from threshold

Inner marker .... between middle marker and threshold

5. **When is the inner marker used?** (AIM 1-1-9)

Ordinarily, there are two marker beacons associated with an ILS, the outer marker (OM) and middle marker (MM). Locations with a Category II ILS also have an inner marker (IM).

6. **While flying a 3° glide slope, which conditions should the pilot expect concerning airspeed, pitch attitude and altitude when encountering a windshear situation where a tailwind shears to a calm or headwind?** (AC 00-54)

Pitch attitude .... Increase

Required thrust .... Reduced, then increased

Vertical speed .... Decreases, then increases

Airspeed............................... Increases, then decreases

Reaction .... Reduce power initially, then increase

7. **While flying a 3° glide slope, which conditions should the pilot expect concerning airspeed, pitch attitude, and altitude when encountering a windshear situation where a headwind shears to a calm or tailwind?** (AC 00-54)

   Pitch attitude .... Decrease
   Required thrust .... Increased, then reduced
   Vertical speed .... Increases
   Airspeed....................................... Decreases, then increases
   Reaction .... Increased power, then a
   decrease in power

8. **Localizers operate within what frequency range?** (AIM 1-1-9)

   Localizers operate on odd tenths within the 108.10 to 111.95 MHz band.

9. **Where is the localizer/transmitter antenna installation located in relation to the runway?** (AIM 1-1-9)

   The antenna is located at the far end of the approach runway.

10. **Where is the glide slope antenna located and what is its normal usable range?** (AIM 1-1-9)

    The glide slope transmitter is located between 750 feet and 1,250 feet from the approach end of the runway (down the runway), and offset 250 feet to 650 feet from it. The glide slope is normally usable to a distance of 10 NM.

11. **What range does a standard localizer have?** (AIM 1-1-9)

    The localizer signal provides course guidance throughout the descent path to the runway threshold from a distance of 18 NM from the antenna site.

12. **What is the angular width of a localizer signal?** (AIM 1 1 0)

    The localizer signal is adjusted to provide an angular width of between 3° to 6°, as necessary to provide a linear width of 700 feet at the runway approach threshold.

13. **What is the normal glide slope angle for a standard ILS?**
(AIM 1-1-9)

The glide path projection angle is normally 3 degrees above horizontal so that it intersects the MM at about 200 feet and the OM at about 1,400 feet above the runway elevation.

14. **What is the sensitivity of a CDI tuned to a localizer signal compared with a CDI tuned to a VOR?**
(FAA-H-8083-15)

Full left or full right deflection occurs at approximately 2.5° from the centerline of a localizer course, which is 4 times greater than when tuned to a VOR, where full-scale deflection equals 10° from the centerline.

15. **Define the term "decision altitude" (DA).** (P/CG)

A specified altitude in the precision approach, charted in feet MSL, at which a missed approach must be initiated if the required visual reference to continue the approach has not been established.

16. **When flying an instrument approach procedure, when can the pilot descend below MDA or DA/DH?**
(14 CFR 91.175)

No pilot may operate an aircraft below the authorized MDA or continue an approach below the authorized DA/DH unless:

a. The aircraft is continuously in a position from which a descent to a landing on the intended runway can be made at a normal rate of descent using normal maneuvers.

b. The flight visibility is not less than the visibility prescribed in the standard instrument approach procedure being used.

c. When at least one of the following visual references for the intended runway is distinctly visible and identifiable to the pilot:

• The approach light system, (except that the pilot may not descend below 100 feet above the touchdown zone elevation using the ALS as a reference unless the red terminating bars or the red side row bars are also distinctly visible and identifiable)

- The threshold
- The threshold markings
- The threshold lights
- REIL
- VASI
- The touchdown zone or touchdown zone markings
- The touchdown zone lights
- The runway or runway markings
- The runway lights

17. What are the legal substitutions for an inoperative outer marker? (14 CFR 91.175)

Compass locator; precision approach radar (PAR) or airport surveillance radar (ASR); DME, VOR, or NDB fixes authorized in the standard instrument approach procedure; or a suitable RNAV system in conjunction with a fix identified in the standard instrument approach procedure.

18. What are PAR and ASR approaches? (AIM 5-4-11)

A PAR approach is a type of radar approach in which a controller provides highly accurate navigational guidance in azimuth and elevation to the pilot (precision approach). An ASR approach is a type of radar approach in which a controller provides navigational guidance in azimuth only (nonprecision approach).

19. What is a "no-gyro" approach? (P/CG and AIM 5-4-11)

A "no-gyro" approach is a radar approach/vector provided in case of a malfunctioning gyro-compass or directional gyro. Instead of providing the pilot with headings to be flown, the controller observes the radar track and issues control instructions "Turn right/left," or "Stop turn," as appropriate.

20. What rate of turn is recommended during execution of a "no-gyro" approach procedure? (AIM 5-4-11)

On a no-gyro approach, all turns should be standard rate until on final; then one-half standard rate on final approach.

21. Are the minimums for an ASR approach expressed as DA or MDA? (AIM 5-4-11)

MDA; Guidance in elevation is not possible but the pilot will be advised when to commence descent to the minimum descent altitude or, if appropriate, to an intermediate step-down fix minimum crossing altitude and subsequently to the prescribed MDA.

22. What is the definition of TDZE? (AIM Glossary)

Touchdown zone elevation (TDZE) is the highest elevation in the first 3,000 feet of the landing surface. TDZE is indicated on the instrument approach procedure chart when straight-in landing minimums are authorized.

C. Nonprecision Approaches

1. What is the definition of the term "nonprecision approach"? (AIM 5-4-5)

A nonprecision approach (NPA) is an instrument approach based on a navigation system that provides course deviation information, but no glidepath deviation information such as VOR, NDB and LNAV.

2. Name the types of nonprecision approach procedures available. (P/CG)

The types of nonprecision approaches available are: LNAV, VOR, TACAN, NDB, LOC, ASR, LDA, and SDF.

3. Define MDA. (P/CG)

The Minimum Descent Altitude is the lowest altitude, expressed in feet above MSL, to which descent is authorized on final approach or during circle-to-land maneuvering, in execution of a standard instrument approach procedure where no electronic glide slope is provided.

4. Define VDP. (P/CG)

Visual Descent Point—a VDP is a defined point on the final approach course of a nonprecision straight-in approach procedure from which normal descent from the MDA to the runway touchdown point may be commenced, provided the approach threshold of that runway, or approach lights or other markings identifiable with the approach end of that runway, are clearly visible to the pilot. Pilots not equipped to receive the VDP should fly the approach procedure as though no VDP had been provided. On an approach chart, a VDP is identified in the profile view by a "V."

5. What is a "VDA"? (AIM 5-4-5)

The vertical descent angle (VDA) provided on non-precision approaches describes a descent angle computed from either the FAF, or a stepdown fix, to the runway threshold at the published TCH. The VDA provides a means for the pilot to establish a stabilized descent from the FAF or stepdown fix to the MDA. The descent angle and TCH information are charted on the profile view of the instrument approach chart following the fix the angle was based on. A stepdown fix is only used as the start point when an angle computed from the FAF would place the aircraft below the stepdown fix altitude. The optimum descent angle is 3.00 degrees and whenever possible the approach will be designed using this angle.

6. Does the VDA guarantee an obstacle protection below the MDA? (AIM 5-4-5)

The published VDA is for information only and is strictly advisory in nature. There is no implicit additional obstacle protection below the MDA. Pilots must still respect the published MDA unless the visual cues stated in 14 CFR §91.175 are present and they can visually acquire and avoid obstacles once below the MDA. The presence of a VDA does not guarantee obstacle protection in the visual segment and does not change any of the requirements for flying a non-precision approach.

7. Will standard instrument approach procedures always have a final approach fix (FAF)? (FAA-H-8261-1)

No. When a FAF is not designated, such as on an approach that incorporates an on-airport VOR or NDB, a final approach point is designated and is typically where the procedure turn intersects the final approach course inbound.

8. If no FAF is published, where does the final approach segment begin on a nonprecision approach? (Order 8260.3B TERPs)

The final approach segment begins where the procedure turn intersects the final approach course inbound.

9. Certain conditions are required for an instrument approach procedure to have "straight-in" minimums published. What are they? (AIM 5-4-20)

Straight-in minimums are shown on the IAP when the final approach course is within 30 degrees of the runway alignment (15 degrees for GPS IAPs) and a normal descent can be made from the IFR altitude shown on the IAP to the runway surface.

10. What is a stepdown fix? (P/CG)

A stepdown fix permits additional descent within a segment of an instrument approach procedure by identifying a point at which a controlling obstacle has been safely overflown.

11. What does a VASI system provide? (AIM 2-1-2)

A VASI system provides visual descent guidance during an approach to a runway; safe obstruction clearance within ±10° of extended runway centerline up to 4 NM from the runway threshold. Two-bar VASI installations normally provide a 3° visual glide path.

12. **What are the major differences between SDF and LDA approaches?** (FAA-H-8083-15)

In an SDF approach procedure, the SDF course may or may not be aligned with the runway; usable off-course indications are limited to 35° either side of course centerline. The SDF signal emitted is fixed at either 6° or 12°.

The LDA compares in utility and accuracy to a localizer, but it is not part of a complete ILS. The LDA course width is between 3° and 6° and thus provides a more precise approach course than an SDF installation. Some LDAs are equipped with a GS. The LDA course is not aligned with the runway, but straight-in minimums may be published where the angle between the runway centerline and the LDA course does not exceed 30°. If this angle exceeds 30°, only circling minimums are published.

13. **What criteria determines whether or not you may attempt an approach?** (14 CFR 91.175)

No regulation states that you cannot attempt an approach, if operating under Part 91 regulations. But if you reach MDA or DH and decide to descend to land, flight visibility must be at least equal to that published.

14. **What regulations require use of specified procedures by all pilots approaching for landing under IFR?** (14 CFR Part 97)

Specified procedures are required by 14 CFR Part 97.

15. **What self-announced radio calls should you make when conducting an instrument approach to an airport without a control tower?** (FAA-H-8261-1)

   a. Initial call within 5–10 minutes of the aircraft's arrival at the IAF with aircraft location and approach intentions.

   b. Departing the IAF, stating the approach that is being initiated.

   c. Procedure turn (or equivalent) inbound.

   d. FAF inbound, stating intended landing runway and maneuvering direction if circling.

   e. Short final, giving traffic on the surface notification of imminent landing.

D. RNAV (GPS) Approaches

1. **Describe the following lines of minima found on area navigation RNAV (GPS) instrument approach charts.** (AIM 5-4-5)

    a. **LNAV**—Lateral navigation only; non-precision approach; requires TSO-C129 (non WAAS) or C145/C146 (WAAS) equipment. Minimums shown as MDA.

    b. **LP**—Localizer Performance; non-precision approach; requires TSO C145/C146 (WAAS) equipment; minimums shown as MDA.

    c. **LNAV/VNAV**—Lateral Nav/Vertical Nav; APV approach; requires approach approved Baro-VNAV or TSO-C145/C146 (WAAS) equipment; minimums are shown as DA.

    d. **LPV**—Localizer performance with vertical guidance; APV approach; requires TSO-C145/C146 (WAAS) equipment; minimums are shown as DA.

    e. **GLS**—GBAS landing system; U.S. version of GBAS is Local Area Augmentation System (LAAS); provides lateral and vertical guidance; requires an aircraft GBAS receiver; relatively new category of approach.

2. **What are "APV" approaches, and give several examples of this type of approach.** (AIM 5-4-5)

    An instrument approach based on a navigation system that is not required to meet the precision approach standards of ICAO Annex 10 but provides course and glidepath deviation information. Examples are: Baro-VNAV, LDA with glidepath, LNAV/VNAV and LPV approaches.

3. **What is indicated when a letter suffix is added to the approach title (i.e., RNAV (GPS) Z RWY 13C)?** (FAA-H-8261-1)

    When two or more straight-in approaches with the same type of guidance exist for a runway, a letter suffix is added to the title of the approach so that it can be more easily identified. These approach charts start with the letter Z and continue in reverse alphabetical order.

4. Will there be any significant differences when two straight-in approaches with the same type of guidance exist for a runway—i.e., RNAV (GPS) Z RWY 13C and RNAV (RNP) Y RWY 13C? (FAA-H-8261-1)

Yes; The approach procedure labeled Z will have lower landing minimums than Y (some older charts may not reflect this). Although both of these approaches can be flown with GPS to the same runway, they can be significantly different—e.g., one may be a "SPECIAL AIRCRAFT & AIRCREW AUTHORIZATION REQUIRED (SAAAR); one can have circling minimums and the other no circling minimums; the minimums are different; and the missed approaches may not be the same.

5. What is a LPV approach? (AIM 1-1-19)

Localizer performance with vertical guidance (LPV) is a type of approach with vertical guidance (APV) that takes advantage of the high accuracy guidance and increased integrity provided by WAAS. This WAAS-generated angular guidance allows the use of the same TERPS approach criteria used for ILS approaches. LPV approaches may have a decision altitude (DA) as low as 200 feet height above touchdown with visibility minimums as low as ½ mile when the terrain and airport infrastructure permit.

6. How can you determine if your aircraft is equipped to fly a LPV approach procedure? (AIM 1-1-19)

GPS/WAAS operation must be conducted in accordance with the FAA-approved aircraft flight manual (AFM) and flight manual supplements. Flight manual supplements will state the level of approach procedure that the receiver supports. IFR-approved WAAS receivers support all GPS only operations as long as lateral capability at the appropriate level is functional.

7. **What does the acronym "LP" indicate in the minimums section of an RNAV (GPS) approach chart?** (AIM 5-4-5)

LP is the acronym for localizer performance. Approaches to LP lines of minima take advantage of the improved accuracy of WAAS to provide approaches with lateral and angular guidance. Angular guidance does not refer to a glideslope angle but rather to the increased lateral sensitivity as the aircraft gets closer to the runway, similar to localizer approaches. LP minimums are only published if terrain, obstructions, or some other reason prevents publishing a vertically guided procedure. LP lines of minima are minimum descent altitudes (MDAs). Also, LP is not a fail-down mode for an LPV. LP and LPV are independent.

8. **After selecting the approach procedure at your destination airport, what method will the GPS receiver use to select the appropriate minimums for the approach?** (AIM 1-1-19)

When an approach procedure is selected and active, the receiver will notify the pilot of the most accurate level of service supported by the combination of the WAAS signal, the receiver, and the selected approach, using the naming conventions on the minima lines of the selected approach procedure. For example, if an approach is published with LPV minima and the receiver is only certified for LNAV/VNAV, the equipment would indicate "LNAV/VNAV available," even though the WAAS signal would support LPV.

9. **What is the significance of temperature limitations published on an approach procedure chart?** (AIM 5-4-5)

A minimum and maximum temperature limitation is published on procedures which authorize Baro-VNAV operation. These temperatures represent the airport temperature above or below which Baro-VNAV is not authorized to LNAV/VNAV minimums.

10. What is the WAAS Channel Number/Approach ID found on the upper left corner of an approach procedure chart used for? (AIM 5-4-5)

The WAAS Channel Number is an optional equipment capability that allows the use of a 5-digit number to select a specific final approach segment without using the menu method.

11. What are the possible reasons your GPS receiver would fail to sequence from the "Armed" to the "Approach" mode prior to the final approach waypoint (FAWP)? (AIM 1-1-18)

The receiver performs a RAIM prediction by 2 NM prior to the FAWP to ensure that RAIM is available at the FAWP as a condition for entering the approach mode. Failure to sequence may be an indication of the detection of a satellite anomaly, failure to arm the receiver (if required), or other problems which preclude completing the approach. The pilot should always ensure that the receiver has sequenced from "Armed" to "Approach" prior to the FAWP (normally occurs 2 NM prior to the FAWP).

12. If the GPS receiver does not sequence from "Armed" to "Approach" mode or a RAIM failure/status annunciation occurs prior to the FAWP, what procedure should the pilot follow? (AIM 1-1-18)

If a RAIM failure/status annunciation occurs prior to the final approach waypoint (FAWP), the approach should not be completed since GPS may no longer provide the required accuracy. The pilot should not descend to minimum descent altitude (MDA), but should proceed to the missed approach waypoint (MAWP) via the FAWP, perform a missed approach, and contact ATC as soon as practical.

13. If a RAIM failure occurs after the FAWP, will the receiver provide a status annunciation to the pilot? (AIM 1-1-18)

The receiver is allowed to continue operating without an annunciation for up to 5 minutes to allow completion of the approach (see receiver operating manual). If the RAIM flag/status annunciation does appear after the FAWP, the missed approach should be executed immediately.

14. **What is the significance of the presence of a gray shaded line from the MDA to the runway in the profile view of a RNAV (GPS) approach?** (FAA-H-8261-1)

It is an indication that the visual segment below the MDA is clear of obstructions on the 34:1 slope. Absence of the gray shaded area indicates the 34:1 OCS is not free of obstructions.

15. **What is indicated when a GPS receiver provides the annunciation "LNAV+V"?** (AC 90-107)

Advisory vertical guidance is being provided. Depending on the manufacturer, some GPS receivers will provide advisory vertical guidance when associated with LP or LNAV lines of minima. The system creates an artificial advisory glide path to assist the pilot in flying a constant descent to the MDA. Barometric altimeter information remains the primary altitude reference for complying with any altitude restrictions.

16. **How will rising terrain be depicted in the plan view of an IAP chart?** (USRGD)

Terrain will be depicted with contour lines in shades of brown in the plan view portion of all IAPs at airports that meet the following criteria:

- If the terrain within the plan view exceeds 4,000 feet above the airport elevation, or

- If the terrain within a 6.0 nautical mile radius of the airport reference point (ARP) rises to at least 2,000 feet above the airport elevation.

17. **What is a computer navigation fix (CNF)?** (AIM 1-1-18)

A point used for the purpose of defining the navigation track for an airborne computer system (i.e., GPS or FMS) is called a computer navigation fix (CNF). CNFs include unnamed DME fixes, beginning and ending points of DME arcs and sensor final approach fixes (FAFs) on some GPS overlay approaches. The CNF five letter name will be enclosed in parenthesis—e.g., "(CFBCD)"

18. **What is the significance of the "negative W" 🅦 symbol placed on some RNAV (GPS) approach charts?** (AIM 1-1-19)

When the approach chart is annotated with the W symbol, site specific WAAS UNRELIABLE NOTAMs or Air Traffic advisories are not provided for outages in WAAS LNAV/VNAV and LPV vertical service. Vertical outages may occur daily at these locations due to being close to the edge of WAAS system coverage. Use LNAV or circling minima for flight planning at these locations, whether as a destination or alternate. For flight operations at these locations, when the WAAS avionics indicate that LNAV/VNAV or LPV service is available, then the vertical guidance may be used to complete the approach using the displayed level of service. If an outage occurs during the procedure, reversion to LNAV minima may be required.

19. **If a discrepancy exists between the information provided by a GPS navigation database and the information published on an approach chart, which one takes precedence?** (AIM 1-1-18)

If significant differences arise between the approach chart and the GPS avionics' application of the navigation database, the published approach chart, supplemented by NOTAMs, holds precedence.

E. Circling Approaches

1. What are circle-to-land approaches? (P/CG)

A circle-to-land approach is not technically an approach, but a maneuver initiated by a pilot to align the aircraft with the runway for landing when a straight-in landing from an instrument approach is not possible or desirable. At tower-controlled airports, this maneuver is made only after ATC authorization has been obtained and the pilot has established required visual reference to the airport.

2. **What is indicated when an approach procedure title (e.g., VOR-A) is followed only by a letter (no runway designation)?** (FAA-H-8083-15)

   The type of approach followed by a letter identifies approaches that do not have straight-in landing minimums and only have circling minimums. The first approach of this type created at the airport is labeled with the letter A, and the lettering continues in alphabetical order (e.g., "VOR-A or "LDA-B").

3. **Why do certain airports have only circling minimums published?** (AIM 5-4-20)

   When either the normal rate of descent or the runway alignment factor of 30 degrees (15 degrees for GPS IAPs) is exceeded, a straight-in minimum is not published and a circling minimum applies.

4. **Can a pilot make a straight-in landing if using an approach procedure having only circling minimums?** (AIM 5-4-20)

   Yes; the fact that a straight-in minimum is not published does not preclude pilots from landing straight-in, if they have the active runway in sight and have sufficient time to make a normal approach to landing. Under such conditions and when ATC has cleared them for landing on that runway, pilots are not expected to circle, even though only circling minimums are published.

5. **If cleared for a "straight-in VOR-DME 34 approach," can a pilot circle to land, if needed?** (P/CG)

   Yes. A "straight-in approach" is an instrument approach wherein final approach is begun without first having executed a procedure turn. Such an approach is not necessarily completed with a straight-in landing or made to straight-in minimums.

6. When can you begin your descent to the runway during a circling approach? (14 CFR 91.175)

Three conditions are required before descent from the MDA can occur:

a. The aircraft is continuously in a position from which a descent to a landing on the intended runway can be made at a normal rate of descent using normal maneuvers.

b. The flight visibility is not less than the visibility prescribed in the standard instrument approach being used.

c. At least one of the specific runway visual references for the intended runway is distinctly visible and identifiable to the pilot.

7. While circling to land you lose visual contact with the runway environment. At the time visual contact is lost, your approximate position is a base leg at the circling MDA. What procedure should be followed? (AIM 5-4-21)

If visual reference is lost while circling to land from an instrument approach, the pilot should make an initial climbing turn toward the landing runway and continue the turn until established on the missed approach course. Since the circling maneuver may be accomplished in more than one direction, different patterns will be required to become established on the prescribed missed approach course, depending on the aircraft position at the time visual reference is lost. Adherence to the procedure will ensure that an aircraft will remain within the circling and missed approach obstacle clearance areas.

8. What obstacle clearance are you guaranteed during a circling approach maneuver? (FAA-H-0261-1)

In all circling approaches, the circling minimum provides 300 feet of obstacle clearance within the circling approach area. The size of this area depends on the category in which the aircraft operates.

Category A .... 1.3-mile radius
Category B .... 1.5-mile radius
Category C .... 1.7-mile radius
Category D .... 2.3-mile radius
Category E .... 4.5-mile radius

9. **What is the significance of the presence of a "negative C" C symbol on the circling line of minima?** (AIM 5-4-20)

Circling approach protected areas developed after late 2012 use the radius distance dependent on aircraft approach category *and* the altitude of the circling MDA which accounts for true airspeed increase with altitude. The approaches using expanded circling approach areas can be identified by the presence of the "negative C" symbol on the circling line of minima.

Note: The increase in size of the circling protected area is particularly beneficial for pilots of CAT C and CAT D turbine-powered, transport category aircraft in that it provides greater lateral obstacle clearance and additional maneuvering room to properly align and stabilize for final approach and landing.

10. **How can a pilot determine the approach category minimums applicable to a particular aircraft?** (AIM 5-4-7)

Minimums are specified for various aircraft approach categories based on a speed of V_{REF}, if specified, or if V_{REF} is not specified, 1.3 V_{S0} at the maximum certified landing weight.

11. **What are the different aircraft approach categories?** (AIM 5-4-7)

Category A...Speed less than 91 knots

Category B...Speed 91 knots or more but less than 121 knots

Category C...Speed 121 knots or more but less than 141 knots

Category D...Speed 141 knots or more but less than 166 knots

Category E...Speed 166 knots or more

12. **An aircraft operating under 14 CFR Part 91 has a 1.3 times V_{S0} speed of 100 KIAS, making Category B minimums applicable. If it becomes necessary to circle at a speed in excess of this category, what minimums should be used?** (AIM 5-4-7)

A pilot must use the minima corresponding to the category determined during certification, or higher. If it is necessary to operate at a speed in excess of the upper limit of the speed range for an aircraft's category, the minimums for the higher category must be used.

F. Missed Approaches

1. **When must a pilot execute a missed approach?** (AIM 5-4-21; 5-5-5)

A missed approach must be executed when one of the following conditions occurs:

a. Arrival at the missed approach point and the runway environment is not yet in sight;

b. Arrival at DA on the glide slope with the runway not yet in sight;

c. Anytime a pilot determines a safe landing is not possible;

d. When circling-to-land visual contact is lost; or

e. When instructed by ATC.

2. **On a nonprecision approach procedure, how is the Missed Approach Point (MAP) determined?** (FAA-H-8083-15)

In nonprecision procedures, the pilot determines the MAP by timing from FAF when the approach aid is well away from the airport, by a fix or NAVAID when the navigation facility is located on the field, or by waypoints as defined by GPS or VOR/DME RNAV.

3. **If no final approach fix is depicted, how is the MAP determined?** (FAA-H-8083-15)

The MAP is at the airport (NAVAID on airport).

4. Where is the MAP on a precision approach?
(FAA-H-8083-15)

For the ILS, the MAP is at the decision altitude/decision height (DA/DH).

5. Under what conditions are missed approach procedures published on an approach chart not followed?
(FAA-H-8083-15)

They are not followed when ATC has assigned alternate missed approach instructions.

6. If, during the execution of an instrument approach procedure, you determine a missed approach is necessary due to full-scale needle deflection, what action is recommended? (AIM 5-4-21)

Protected obstacle clearance areas for missed approach are predicated on the assumption that the missed approach is initiated at the decision altitude/height (DA/H) or at the missed approach point, and not lower than minimum descent altitude (MDA). Reasonable buffers are provided for normal maneuvers. However, no consideration is given to an abnormally early turn. Therefore when an early missed approach is executed, pilots should (unless otherwise cleared by ATC) fly the IAP as specified on the approach plate to the missed approach point at or above the MDA or DA/H, before executing a turning maneuver.

7. What action should a pilot take in the event a balked (rejected) landing occurs at a position other than the published missed approach point? (AIM 5-4-21)

The pilot should contact ATC as soon as possible to obtain an amended clearance. If unable to contact ATC for any reason, the pilot should attempt to re-intercept a published segment of the missed approach and comply with route and altitude instructions. If unable to contact ATC, and in the pilot's judgment it is no longer appropriate to fly the published missed approach procedure, then the pilot should consider either maintaining visual conditions if practicable and reattempt a landing, or a circle-climb over the airport. Contact ATC when able to do so.

8. **What are several factors a pilot should consider (prior to the approach) when assessing options available if it becomes necessary to execute a missed approach from beyond the MAP or below the MDA or DA/DH?** (AIM 5-4-21)

The pilot should consider factors such as the aircraft's geographical location with respect to the prescribed missed approach point, direction of flight, and/or minimum turning altitudes in the prescribed missed approach procedure. The pilot must also consider aircraft performance, visual climb restrictions, charted obstacles, availability of a published obstacle departure procedure, takeoff visual climb requirements as expressed by nonstandard takeoff minima, other traffic expected to be in the vicinity, or other factors not specifically expressed by the approach procedures.

9. **What is a low approach?** (AIM 4-3-12)

A low approach (sometimes referred to as a low pass) is the go-around maneuver following an approach. Instead of landing or making a touch and go, a pilot may wish to go-around (low approach) in order to expedite a particular operation (a series of practice instrument approaches is an example). Unless otherwise authorized by ATC, the low approach should be made straight ahead, with no turns or climb made until the pilot has made a thorough visual check for other aircraft in the area.

10. **What does the phrase "Cleared for the Option" mean?** (AIM 4-3-22)

The "Cleared for the Option" procedure will permit an instructor, flight examiner or pilot the option to make a touch-and-go, low approach, missed approach, stop-and-go, or full stop landing. The pilot should make a request for this procedure passing the final approach fix inbound on an instrument approach.

G. Landing Procedures

1. **Is it legal to land a civil aircraft if the actual visibility is below the minimums published on the approach chart?** (14 CFR 91.175)

   No, 14 CFR Part 91 states that no pilot operating an aircraft, except a military aircraft of the U.S., may land that aircraft when the flight visibility is less than the visibility prescribed in the standard instrument approach procedure being used.

2. **When landing at an airport with an operating control tower following an IFR flight, must the pilot call FSS to close the flight plan?** (AIM 5-1-15)

   No, if operating on an IFR flight plan to an airport with a functioning control tower, the flight plan will automatically be closed upon landing.

3. **You are operating on an IFR flight plan into an airport without an operating control tower, and have forgotten to close your flight plan after landing. Discuss the effect this will have on ATC.** (AIM 5-1-15)

   The airspace surrounding that airport cannot be released for use by other IFR aircraft until the status of your flight has been determined.

4. **If the visibility provided by ATC is less than that prescribed for the approach, can a pilot legally continue an approach and land?** (FAA-H-8083-15)

   According to 14 CFR Part 91, no pilot may land when the flight visibility is less than the visibility prescribed in the standard IAP being used. ATC will provide the pilot with the current visibility reports appropriate to the runway in use. This may be in the form of prevailing visibility, runway visual value (RVV), or runway visual range (RVR). However, only the pilot can determine if the flight visibility meets the landing requirements indicated on the approach chart. If the flight visibility meets the minimum prescribed for the approach, then the approach may be continued to a landing. If the flight visibility is less than that prescribed for the approach, then the pilot must execute a missed approach, regardless of the reported visibility.

H. Instrument Approach Procedure Charts: General

All questions in this section reference government AeroNav charts.

1. **When the approach procedure title contains more than one navigational system separated by a slash (e.g., VOR/ DME 31), what does this indicate?** (AIM 5-4-5)

   It indicates that more than one type of equipment must be used to execute the final approach.

2. **When the approach procedure title contains more than one navigational system separated by the word "or" (e.g., VOR or GPS RWY 15), what does this indicate?** (AIM 5-4-5)

   It indicates that either type of equipment may be used to execute the final approach (e.g., VOR or GPS RWY 15).

3. **With no FAF available, when would final descent to the published MDA be started?** (FAA-H-8083-15)

   For non-precision approaches, a final descent is initiated and the final segment begins at either the FAF or the final approach point (FAP). When no FAF is depicted, the final approach point is the point at which the aircraft is established inbound on the final approach course.

4. **What significance does a black triangle with a white "A" appearing in the Notes section of an approach chart, have to a pilot?** (FAA-H-8083-15, TERPs)

   It indicates that nonstandard IFR alternate minimums exist for the airport. If an "NA" appears after the "A," alternate minimums are not authorized. This information is found in the beginning of the TPP. Approved terminal weather observation and reporting facilities, or a general area weather report, must be available before an airport may serve as an alternate.

5. What is the significance of the term "radar required" found on some approach charts? (P/CG)

A term displayed on charts and approach plates and included in FDC NOTAMs to alert pilots that segments of either an instrument approach procedure or a route are not navigable because of either the absence or unusability of a NAVAID. The pilot can expect to be provided radar navigational guidance while transiting segments labeled with this term.

For the following sections I.–M., refer to the ILS or LOC RWY 16 approach chart for Fort Worth, Texas, depicted on page 4-39.

I. Instrument Approach Procedure Charts: Plan View

1. What are the MSAs for this approach? (FAA-H-8083-15)

2,200 feet .... 180° through 270°
3,600 feet .... 270° through 360°
2,800 feet .... 360° through 180°

2. On which facility is the MSA centered, and what does it provide? (AIM 5-4-5)

The MSA is centered on the MUFIN LOM; the altitude shown provides at least 1,000 feet of clearance above the highest obstacle within the defined sector up to a distance of 25 NM from the facility. Navigational course guidance is not assured at the MSA.

3. What is the IAF for this procedure? (FAA-H-8083-15)

The IAF is MUFIN LOM.

4. What significance does the bold arrow extending from Bowie VOR have? (FAA-H-8083-15)

It represents a feeder route or flyable route utilized when transitioning from the enroute structure to the initial approach fix.

5. **When intercepting the localizer from procedure turn inbound, what will be the relative bearing on the ADF indicator as the localizer needle begins to center?** (FAA-H-8083-15)

Assuming a 45° intercept angle, the relative bearing will be 315°.

6. **What are the frequencies for the locator outer marker and middle marker beacons?** (FAA-H-8083-15)

The locator frequency is 365 kHz. All marker beacons transmit on a frequency of 75 MHz.

7. **Explain the difference between a "Note" such as RADAR REQUIRED or ADF REQUIRED being charted in the plan view of an approach procedure, and a note being charted in the "Notes" box of the pilot briefing portion of the approach chart.** (AIM 5-4-5)

When radar or other equipment is required for procedure entry from the enroute environment, a note will be charted in the plan view of the approach procedure chart. When radar or other equipment is required on portions of the procedure outside the final approach segment, including the missed approach, a note will be charted in the notes box of the pilot briefing portion of the approach chart. Notes are not charted when VOR is required outside the final approach segment. Pilots should ensure that the aircraft is equipped to receive the required NAVAID(s) in order to execute the approach, including the missed approach.

8. **Where does the final approach segment begin for the ILS 16 approach?** (FAA-H-8083-15)

On all precision approaches, the final approach segment begins when the glide slope is intercepted at glide slope altitude. For non-precision approaches such as the straight-in LOC 16 approach, the final approach segment begins at the Maltese cross which is the MUFIN LOM.

J. Instrument Approach Procedure Charts: Profile

1. Within what distance from the MUFIN LOM must the procedure turn be executed? (FAA-H-8083-15)

The procedure turn must be executed within 10 NM.

2. If a procedure turn is required, what would be the minimum altitude while flying this segment? (FAA-H-8083-15)

The minimum altitude for the initial approach segment and while executing the procedure turn is 2,400 feet MSL.

3. To what altitude may a pilot descend after the procedure turn? (FAA-H-8083-15)

When established inbound after the procedure turn, the pilot may descend to 2,000 MSL.

4. What does the number "1992" located at the outer marker indicate? (FAA-H-8083-15)

1992 indicates the altitude of the glide slope at the outer marker.

5. What is the glide slope angle for this approach? (FAA-H-8083-15)

The glide slope angle is 3°.

6. What is the altitude at which the electronic glide slope crosses the threshold of runway 16? (FAA-H-8083-15)

Threshold crossing height (TCH) is 57 feet.

7. **If the glide slope became inoperative, could you continue this approach if established on the localizer at the time of the malfunction? Why?** (FAA-H-8083-15)

Yes, provided ATC is notified and approves a localizer-only approach. Since the procedure indicates a localizer-only minimum, a localizer-only approach can be authorized. The minimum is now an MDA and the approach is now a nonprecision procedure with MAP being a time or DME point.

8. **If you discovered your marker beacon receiver was inoperative, what are the authorized substitutes for the MUFIN outer marker?** (FAA-H-8083-15)

Substitutes for the outer marker are:

a. The compass locator (365 kHz)

b. 5.3 DME I-FTW

c. Maverick VORTAC (TTT) radial 269

9. **What DME distance is indicated in the profile view for the MUFIN LOM and the runway threshold?** (FAA-H-8083-15)

The MUFIN LOM is 5.3 NM, and the runway threshold is 1.5 NM from the localizer antenna site.

10. **Where is the MAP for the precision and nonprecision approach in this procedure?** (FAA-H-8083-15)

a. For the precision approach procedure, the MAP is upon reaching the DH of 910 feet MSL on the glide slope.

b. For the nonprecision procedure, the MAP is:
   • 1.5 DME from IFTW; or
   • Time from MUFIN.

K. Instrument Approach Procedure Charts: Minimums

1. **What is the minimum visibility for a Category A full ILS 16 approach?** (FAA-H-8083-15)

   Minimum visibility is ½ mile or RVR of 2,400 feet. RVR of 1,800 feet is authorized with the use of FD or AP or HUD to DA.

2. **If the approach light system became inoperative, how would you determine the minimum visibility for a Category A full ILS 16 approach?** (FAA-H-8083-15)

   To determine landing minimums when components or aids of the system are inoperative or are not utilized, inoperative components or visual aids tables are published and normally appear in the front section of NACO approach chart books.

3. **Convert the following RVR values to meteorological visibility.** (14 CFR 91.175)

RVR (feet)	Statute miles
1,600	1/4
2,400	1/2
3,200	5/8
4,000	3/4
4,500	7/8
5,000	1
6,000	1-1/4

4. **Are takeoff minimums standard or nonstandard for Ft. Worth Meacham Field?** (FAA-H-8083-15)

   Nonstandard; takeoff minimums are not standard and/or departure procedures are published as indicated by the triangle with a "T" printed in the notes area. IFR Takeoff Minimums and (Obstacle) Departure Procedures Section, Section L, of the Terminal Procedures Publications (TPPs) should be consulted.

5. **For the localizer approach 16, what are the minimums for a Category A airplane if a circling maneuver is desired?** (FAA-H-8083-15)

The circling MDA is 1,260 MSL; the visibility requirement increases to 1 mile for the circling maneuver.

6. **What significance do the numbers in parentheses (200-½) have?** (FAA-H-8083-15)

Any minimums found in parentheses are not applicable to civil pilots. These minimums are directed at military pilots who should refer to appropriate regulations.

7. **When established at the MDA on the final approach course inbound for the straight-in LOC 16 approach, is the MDA expressed as Height Above Touchdown (HAT) or Height Above Airport (HAA)?** (FAA-H-8083-15)

The MDA of 530 feet for a straight-in landing always represents height above touchdown (HAT) since the approach is for a specific runway. MDAs for circling approaches will always represent height above airport (HAA) since a specific runway will not be used for landing.

8. **If the current weather reports indicate ceilings 100 overcast and visibility ½ mile, can a pilot legally make an approach to ILS 16, and can he land?** (FAA-H-8083-15)

Under 14 CFR Part 91, the approach may be attempted regardless of the ceiling and visibility. At the DA (DH) the pilot must have the runway environment in sight and have the prescribed flight visibility to land. If these conditions are met, the approach may be continued to a landing.

L. Instrument Approach Procedure Charts: Aerodrome

1. What types of lighting are available for runway 16? (FAA-H-8083-15)

HIRL—High-intensity runway lighting

MALSR—Medium-intensity approach lighting system with sequenced flashing lights; denoted by the circled A5 on the approach to runway 16.

2. What is the touchdown zone elevation for runway 16? (FAA-H-8083-15)

The TDZE is 710 MSL.

3. What is the bearing and distance of the MAP from the FAF? (FAA-H-8083-15)

The MAP is 164°, 3.8 NM from FAF for the localizer approach, and approximately the same distance for the full ILS approach.

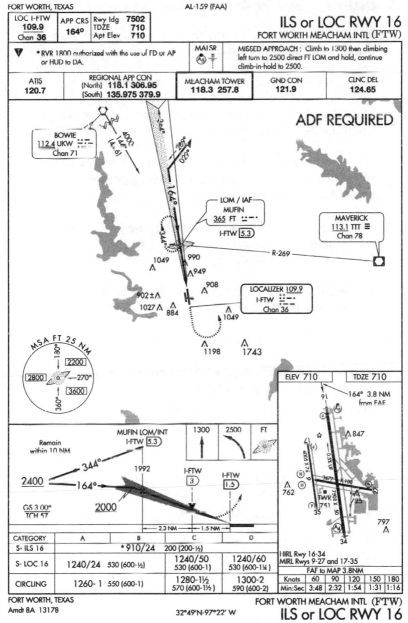

ILS or LOC RWY 16
FORT WORTH MEACHAM INTL (FTW)

FORT WORTH, TEXAS

AL-159 (FAA)

| LOC I-FTW 109.9 Chan 36 | APP CRS 164° | Rwy Idg 7502 TDZE 710 Apt Elev 710 |

▼ * RVR 1800 authorized with the use of FD or AP or HUD to DA.

MALSR

MISSED APPROACH : Climb to 1300 then climbing left turn to 2500 direct FT LOM and hold, continue climb-in-hold to 2500.

| ATIS 120.7 | REGIONAL APP CON (North) 118.1 306.95 (South) 135.975 379.9 | MEACHAM TOWER 118.3 257.8 | GND CON 121.9 | CLNC DEL 124.65 |

ADF REQUIRED

CATEGORY	A	B	C	D
S- ILS 16		* 910/24 200 (200-½)		
S- LOC 16	1240/24 530 (600-½)		1240/50 530 (600-1)	1240/60 530 (600-1¼)
CIRCLING	1260- 1 550 (600-1)		1280-1½ 570 (600-1½)	1300-2 590 (600-2)

HIRL Rwy 16-34
MIRL Rwys 9-27 and 17-35
FAF to MAP 3.8NM

Knots	60	90	120	150	180
Min:Sec	3:48	2:32	1:54	1:31	1:16

FORT WORTH, TEXAS
Amdt 8A 13178

32°49'N-97°22' W

FORT WORTH MEACHAM INTL (FTW)
ILS or LOC RWY 16

Additional Study Questions

1. What is the function of the "high" and "low" setting on the marker beacon receiver? (AFM)

2. You have arrived at decision altitude on a precision approach and only have the approach light system in sight. Must you execute a missed approach or can you continue? (14 CFR 91.175)

3. How do you determine flight visibility when transitioning from IMC to visual on an instrument approach procedure? (FAA-H-8083-15)

4. Are the required visibility figures in the instrument minimums sections on approach charts statute or nautical? (FAA-H-8083-15)

5. The acronym LAHSO refers to what specific ATC procedure? (AIM 4-3-11)

6. What is a side-step maneuver? (FAA-H-8083-15)

7. Be capable of locating and defining the following approach chart abbreviations:

ALS	HIRL	MALS	SDF
ALSF	IAF	MAP	TAA
APV	IM	MDA	TCH
BC	LDA	NA	TDZE
DA	LDIN	NoPT	TDZL
DH	LNAV/VNAV	OM	VDA
FAF	LOM	RCLS	VDP
GLS	LP	RNP	WP/WPT
HAA	LPV	RVR	
HAT	LR	S	

8. Define the term, "final approach point." (AIM Glossary)

Scenario-Based Training

5

by Arlynn McMahon

Introduction

During the oral portion of the instrument practical exam, expect the questions to include scenarios focused on the flight environment that instrument pilots are authorized to fly in. The examiner/inspector will expect you to be able to anticipate weather changes during flight and how the flight handling characteristics of an aircraft may change with changes in meteorological conditions. You should also expect questions that find you unexpectedly in conditions that you must escape from—primarily icing, fog and thunderstorms.

Often there is more than one correct answer for a scenario-based question; therefore, ensure that your answers to the examiner include the content identified as the "must" items listed in the answers given below. Additionally, be generous in displaying to the examiner your aeronautical decision making by sharing your thought process aloud as you analyze the elements involved.

As a pilot with an instrument rating, you are expected by the FAA, the industry, and your future passengers to handle the unexpected as well as routine procedures. You must see the "big picture" in addition to the details. In answering oral exam questions, you must look for and recognize the underlying elements presented by the scenarios. Be prepared to include risk management aspects in your answers whenever possible.

Scenario-Based Questions

1. **On a beautiful clear, sunny, VMC day, you are flying on an IFR flight plan. Are you required to be instrument current?**

   In this question, the examiner is testing your knowledge of meteorological conditions versus the rules under which you are flying.

   Regardless of the meteorological conditions, if I am flying under instrument rules, then I must be instrument current.

2. **Thirty minutes after takeoff you enter the clouds. The climb through a cloud layer requires 10 minutes. The enroute phase is 50 minutes and is above the overcast layer, at night. Descent requires 30 minutes through the clouds before breaking out into clear VMC. How much of this flight will you log as "actual instruments"?**

   Your answer must include the regulation pertaining to logging time. In this scenario, the flight through the clouds obviously should be logged; however, the examiner has allowed you to judge if the flight above an overcast layer at night is "by reference to instruments."

   I would log as "actual instruments" all of the time that I was flying by reference to instruments. This would obviously include the time flying through the cloud layer, but also any other time that I was flying by reference to instruments. *[See page 1-5, #A.6, A.8]*

3. **Your aircraft is equipped with a certified GPS, but during the VOT preflight check, both VORs failed to be accurate. You have no other means of navigation. How will this affect your flight?**

   Your answer must demonstrate your knowledge of a VOT check and the accuracy requirements (see page 2-10), as well as your knowledge of GPS requirements.

   I will not be able to file an IFR flight plan. To file an IFR flight plan, I must have an alternate (non-GPS) means of navigation unless my GPS is WAAS certified.

4. **The airport that you desire to use as a required alternate airport offers only RNAV IAPs. How will this affect you?**

If an alternate airport is required and that airport offers only RNAV IAPs, then my aircraft must be equipped with a WAAS-certified GPS. If there are IAPs that use other NAVAIDs, in addition to the RNAV IAP, then I can file it as a required alternate with a GPS that is not WAAS certified.

The following questions refer to the enroute low-altitude chart for the Lexington, Kentucky, area shown on the next page.

5. **On a flight departing from the Cynthiana Harrison Co Airport to Georgetown Scott County Field, when do FARs require you to be on an IFR flight plan?**

I must be on an IFR flight plan when conditions are less than VMC and when in controlled airspace, which in the Cynthiana area is 1,200 feet AGL, and in the vicinity of Georgetown is 700 feet AGL.

6. **During the preflight run-up, you find the transponder is INOP. How does this affect your IFR flight from Cynthiana to Georgetown?**

- Transponder requirements are not specific to flights under IFR.

- Technically, the flight from Cynthiana to Georgetown is not in airspace that requires a transponder: it's not in or above Class C or Class B airspace and I'm flying below 10,000 feet MSL. So from that perspective I am legal to fly.

- However, the inoperative equipment regulation would require me to placard the transponder INOP.

- With the unit INOP, I will leave the transponder unit OFF.

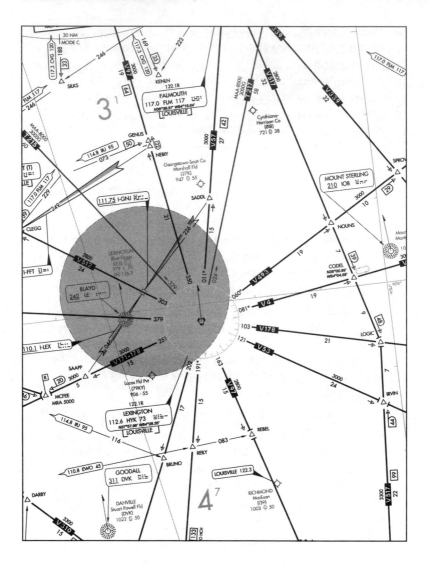

7. **Your flight plan is a round-robin: Depart KLEX, direct to HYK, V53 IRVIN, V517 LOGIC, V178 HYK, landing KLEX. You filed 3,000 feet MSL. Your ATC clearance is: "Cleared as filed, climb to and maintain 2,500' expect 3,000' 10 minutes after..." Immediately after takeoff, you are IMC with no ground contact and very shortly after that all calls to ATC go unanswered. You hear no other traffic on the frequency. What will you do?**

Your answer must demonstrate your understanding of IFR 2-way communications loss. It should demonstrate your ability to diagnose routine radio problems. Your answer could include:

* I will climb to 2,500 feet MSL and proceed direct to HYK. After 10 minutes or upon crossing HYK, I will climb to 3,000 feet. At IRVINE I'll climb to 3,300 feet, and at LOGIC I'll descend to 3,000 feet to HYK.

* I'll change my transponder code to 7600 and I'll continue to make radio calls into the blind.

* In the meantime, I'll try to correct or work around the problem by:
  1. Verifying the volume control.
  2. Verifying the audio panel receive/transmit selector.
  3. Verifying the headset is fully connected.
  4. Attempting to call ATC using the other COM.
  5. Attempting to call ATC using the co-pilot PTT.
  6. Attempting to call Louisville FSS using the HYK RCO and relaying to ATC.
  7. Attempting to use my cell phone to call FSS, who may be able to relay to ATC for me.

* Considering what I think is the active runway and the IAP most likely to result in seeing the runway, I'll choose an appropriate approach procedure, and if necessary, I will hold in order to depart the IAP as close to my flight plan time as possible.

8. **When using VOR as the primary source for navigation, how will you set up your NAVs along this flight (i.e., Which NAV will you set up to identify each intersection)?**

Good instrument pilots have "standard operating procedures" that they use consistently. The examiner would like to know you have developed SOPs. Your answer could be:

My cockpit standard operating procedure is to always use NAV #1 to navigate along and NAV #2 to identify intersections. So I'd put:

* HYK in #1 and the NAVAID 44 NM south in #2 to identify IRVINE.

* Then turning to navigate along V517: The NAVAID 44 NM south in #1 and HYK in #2 to identify LOGIC.

* Make a turn at LOGIC: The NAVAID 48 NM north in #1 and HYK in #2 to identify CODEL and NOUNS.

* Then turning to navigate along V493, I'd probably put HYK in #2 in anticipation of using #1 for the IAP.

9. **When using GPS as a primary source for navigation, you would enter each intersection as a waypoint into the GPS Flight Plan: KLEX, HYK, IRVIN, LOGIC, CODEL, NOUNS, HYK, KLEX. What is the button sequence to remove CODEL from the flight plan?**

Your answer will depend on your specific GPS unit; you should demonstrate your understanding of your GPS unit by describing the particular button sequence required to remove the CODEL waypoint.

10. During this flight, what tasks are needed to properly prepare for an IAP?

Your answer should demonstrate your understanding of the tasks to prepare for an IFR arrival, and your ability to prioritize and manage tasks. Your specific answer will depend on your airplane, but should include specific tasks and the timing for each. For example:

To properly prepare for an IAP, I would:

• Listen to the ATIS.

• Self-brief the approach procedure by reviewing the IAP in detail.

• Reduce speed.

• Set up avionics and identify NAVAIDs.

• Perform the pre-landing checklist and configure the aircraft for landing.

11. Will the length of runway required for a landing from an IAP be different than a landing from a VFR approach?

Most pilots configure the aircraft and fly an IAP differently than a VFR approach. The examiner is testing your standard operating procedure and your understanding of how that may affect your runway requirements. Your answer could include:

• The landing should be a full-stall touchdown, especially from an IAP when snow or standing water may be present on the runway.

• If I fly an IAP at a speed that is higher than the manufacturer's recommended VFR approach speed, it will require more runway to land to give the plane time to dissipate the excess speed.

• If I have a stabilized approach set up, I might land from an IAP with less than full flaps, which will require more runway to land.

12. The PTS calls for our IAPs to be "stabilized approaches." Why is that important and what does having a stabilized approach mean to you?

Your answer must demonstrate your knowledge of the elements of the stabilized approach for your specific airplane and the relationship between a stabilized approach and CFIT-related accidents. Your answer could include:

It's important to have a stabilized approach during final descent because I don't want last-minute configuration changes or distractions. This is important in preventing CFIT accidents. My stabilized approach means that I'll achieve by 1,000 feet AGL (or nearly after) the FAF and continue to touchdown with:

- proper configuration for landing.
- an appropriate power setting.
- A consistent 500–700 fpm rate of descent (if nonprecision approach).
- stabilized approach airspeed for the lowest possible landing category.
- tracking on-course, within one dot.
- on or within one-dot-above glideslope (if precision approach).
- only minor corrections. If large corrections are necessary, then I'll miss the approach rather than continue a descent or attempt to salvage a risky situation.

13. If you encounter unforecasted freezing rain, would you allow the autopilot to control the plane or would you hand-fly it?

There is no "right" answer to this question. The examiner wants to know that you have given thought to how you will handle this situation. Possible answers:

AGAINST using the autopilot: I would hand fly. The largest hazard in freezing rain is that ice accumulates quickly on the aircraft surface and results in a loss of lift. If flying with the autopilot on, I won't receive tactile inputs on the effectiveness of control surfaces and may not perceive the loss of lift.

FOR using the autopilot: I would turn on the autopilot. This represents a busy time in the cockpit. I have to alter plans and reprogram technology. I want the autopilot to relieve some of the workload tasks.

14. **If you were concerned about freezing rain developing along your flight, what specific weather reports or forecasts would you look at to determine the likelihood of freezing rain developing?**

Several of the forecasts may mention freezing rain. However, I know that freezing rain is the result of a temperature inversion. The Winds and Temperatures Aloft Forecast shows air temperatures at various altitudes; I could use this forecast to detect a temperature inversion—to see if there is warm air over colder air and temperatures near freezing.

15. **If you inadvertently encounter freezing rain, what would be your preferred escape method?**

Your answer must demonstrate your understanding of the impact of operating in freezing rain. It could include:

- An immediate escape is necessary—I would not wait.

- The best and fastest escape from freezing rain is a 180-degree turn back to where I came from.

- The next best escape method is to try to change altitudes to find warmer air.

16. **Do you have any anti-ice or deice equipment installed on your airplane?**

Your answer must be specific to your airplane; demonstrate that you know what equipment is installed on your airplane as well as when to use it.

- Alternate air control—used when primary air input is blocked; allows entry of heated air.

- Carburetor heat—used to keep fuel and air flowing to the engine. I would turn it on after the first sign of possible carburetor icing.

Continued

- Pitot heat—used to keep the pilot/static instrument operational. I would turn it on in advance of a possible icing situation.

- Windshield defrost—used to keep the windshield clear. I would turn it on in advance of a possible icing situation.

17. If you encounter icing during a lost-com situation, what will you do?

This is not a question about lost-com procedures. Your answer must demonstrate your awareness of a possible emergency situation forming and how you will handle it.

- This is no longer just a lost-com situation, but is now a possible emergency.

- I will change the transponder code from 7600 to 7700.

- I will use my pilot's emergency prerogative. I will do whatever I feel I need to do—including changing altitudes to get out of the clouds or to find warm air, changing route segment, and/or initiating an IAP to the nearest airport.

18. If you are concerned about fog, what specific weather reports/forecasts would you look at to determine the likelihood of fog developing?

Your answer should demonstrate your knowledge of the contents of specific reports and forecasts. (Refer to Chapter 1, Section H.) Specifically:

- I would review all of the reports for current temperatures and dewpoints.

- I would consider how the setting sun (if flying in the evening) or rising sun (early in the morning) might change the temperature.

- If the temperature and dewpoint spread is becoming small, then I know to expect fog.

19. If you inadvertently encounter thick fog, what would be your preferred escape method?

Your answer should demonstrate your understanding of fog.

Flying in fog is not usually a problem until it becomes time for an IAP and landing. Depending on the type of fog:

- I would look for an airport at a higher elevation, or if it's upslope fog, I might look for an airport at a lower elevation.

- If flying near the coast, I would look for an airport further inland.

- If all else fails, I would lean the engine for best economy and fly to an area with improved conditions.

20. A VOR IAP has a published MSA. An RNAV IAP has a published TAA? How do you correctly use these altitudes?

Your answer must demonstrate an understanding of the difference between these altitudes.

- A minimum safe altitude (MSA) is advisory information used as an emergency quick reference. Pilots normally don't use the MSA during normal operations. An MSA may be published on any IAP.

- A terminal arrival area (TAA) is only associated with an RNAV IAP. The TAA is part of the IAP. If I am in a TAA and have been cleared for the IAP, I am considered to be on a published portion of the IAP and am authorized to descend to that altitude without further ATC instructions.

21. While conducting a nonprecision IAP, you decide that you are too high. At what point can you initiate a missed approach procedure?

Your answer must demonstrate your understanding of the missed approach procedure.

I can arrest my descent at any time. However, I must continue the IAP to the missed approach point before maneuvering.

22. You are flying an airway that has three altitudes published for that segment:

8,000
5,000G
4,500*

What does this mean to you?

- 8,000 is the minimum enroute altitude (MEA) if the aircraft is not GPS equipped.

- 5,000G is the altitude that may be used as the MEA when navigating via GPS.

- 4,500* is the minimum obstruction clearance altitude (MOCA); ATC may assign this altitude when I'm within 22 NM of the VOR.

23. About 25 NM from your destination, you determine that the aircraft has been using more fuel than planned. You think you should have adequate fuel to reach your destination as long as there are no delays. Is this something that you should report to ATC?

Yes, I should inform ATC so that they can be a resource for me. Additionally:

- I should report "minimum fuel" when I'm concerned about the time in my tanks.

- I would declare a "fuel emergency" if I need priority handling to the airport.

- I would not hesitate to declare an emergency. I would not be concerned about possible repercussions, because it's better to be safe than sorry.

24. You have checked out in the flight school's new C172; how will you conduct an IFR preflight instrument cockpit check?

- I would verify that all needed cockpit equipment (charts, flashlight, etc.) is on board and accessible in the cockpit. Verifying means touching everything, and not just assuming that items are in my flight bag.

- I would verify the instruments are reading correctly for ground operations:

  1. Magnetic compass is full of fluid and free. During taxi, it swings appropriately to known headings.

  2. Airspeed indicator reads zero.

  3. Attitude indicator is stable and horizon bar is set correctly.

  4. Altimeter reads field elevation when set to current barometric pressure.

  5. Baro setting may also be needed in GPS, autopilot or other technology.

  6. Turn coordinator indicates correctly during taxi and the ball rolls away from the turn.

  7. HI/HSI/RMI is set correctly and moves correctly during taxi.

  8. VSI indicates near zero.

25. During the instrument cockpit check, you note the following:

- **The turn coordinator does not indicate a turn during taxi.**
- **With the correct barometric pressure set, the altimeter reads 60 feet above the field elevation.**
- **Vertical speed is showing a 100-foot climb on the ground.**

Which of the indications listed represent a no-go item and which are acceptable?

No-go items:

- The turn coordinator does not indicate a turn during taxi.

- Vertical speed is showing a 100-foot climb on the ground.

Acceptable:

- With the correct barometric pressure set, the altimeter reads 60 feet above the field elevation.

26. During your first flight in the flight school's new C172, what equipment checks will you perform for an IFR flight that you normally don't do on a VFR flight?

Your answer should demonstrate your knowledge of the equipment checks that are appropriate for your plane.

I would perform the following equipment checks:

- Verify that the pitot-static check has been completed in the previous 24 months.

- During preflight inspection, check the pitot heat.

- Turn on all equipment. Make sure that it powers up correctly.

- During run-up, in addition to all normal checklist items, I would:
  1. Perform an autopilot check.
  2. Verify that the VOR(s) have been checked and appropriately noted in the previous 30 days.
  3. Set the clock and confirm its operation.
  4. Verify the outside air temperature.
  5. Follow the proper GPS startup and check procedures. Verify the database expiration date and RAIM.

27. What action would you take if you encounter unforecasted rime ice?

Your answer must include an understanding of the formation of rime ice, as well as strategies you would use to escape the icing conditions and improve your situation.

Rime ice forms when flying in visible moisture and the outside air temperature is at or below freezing. My highest priority is to get to conditions that remove one of these factors. Specifically, I would consider:

- Doing something immediately. I would not delay; rime ice forms quickly.

- Inform ATC that I'm encountering ice. Then based on my knowledge of current weather conditions:
  1. Change altitudes to get out of the clouds.
  2. Change altitudes to get to warmer air.

3. Make a 180-degree turn. If I was not picking up ice where I came from, then I would go back there.

4. Land as soon as possible.

I would use additional strategies to improve my situation:

* Turn on anti-ice equipment (pitot heat, windshield defrost, carb heat, etc.).

* As time permits: Solicit PIREPs from ATC from other pilots in my vicinity regarding their icing conditions.

28. After inadvertently encountering icing conditions, your engine begins to run rough, with a loss of engine RPM. What is the likely cause and solution?

Your answer must include an understanding of the engine and symptoms associated with engine roughness in icing conditions. Specifically:

* Probability is high that my engine air intake has become blocked.

* If my engine is equipped with carb heat, I would apply it to access outside air through a different inlet.

* If my engine is equipped with alternate air, I would turn it on to access outside air through a different inlet.

* I would exit icing conditions as soon as possible.

29. On a day IMC flight, about 50 miles from your destination, you notice the ammeter is discharging. What will you do?

Your answer must include an understanding of the electrical system and the underlying implication of an ammeter discharging.

I am about to lose electrical power and with it, electrical accessories. If faced with this situation, I would:

* Recycle the master switch (alternator side on a split switch) to reset a possible overvoltage relay problem.

* Prepare for possible complete electrical failure.

* Turn off all unnecessary electrical equipment.

* Inform ATC, if I still have communications.

Continued

- Not count on making my destination. I would select the closest airport with an IAP that will assure a successful approach.
- Navigate to the closest IAF.
- Obtain the POH and review electrical system checklists.
- Inform passengers of the situation and how they may be of assistance to me.

30. When I say that I want to see strong SRM habits in the cockpit during this flight, specifically what does that mean I want you to do?

Your answer must demonstrate your understanding of SRM and its six components.

Single-pilot resource management (SRM) consists of six components that are closely affected by each other. Specifically:

1. *Aeronautical Decision Making (ADM)* —you want to know that I have looked at all the available options and made a decision based on facts and my personal limitations.

2. *Risk Management (RM)* —you want to know that my decisions are made in such a way to mitigate risks.

3. *Task Management (TA)* —you want to see me prioritize and plan cockpit workload so that I don't become saturated with tasks and fail to aviate, navigate and communicate.

4. *Situational Awareness (SA)* —you want to see that I have an awareness of what is going on inside and outside of the airplane, presently as well as how the situation may develop during the remainder of the flight.

5. *Controlled Flight into Terrain (CFIT)* —you want to see me flying in such a way that reduces the likelihood that we'll fly into terrain. This probably means that I have demonstrated good ADM, RM, TA and SA.

6. *Automation Management (AM)* —you want to see me managing a current level of automation and being aware of automation modes, alerts and programming.

31. Give me a few specific examples of how you use good task management skills on an IFR flight?

Your answer should demonstrate your understanding of how to plan for and prioritize tasks.

- I'll prioritize tasks in a way that doesn't distract from flying the airplane. Overall, this means that I will Aviate first; Navigate second; Communicate third.

- I'll execute tasks (such as checklists) so as not to increase workload during critical phases of flight.

- I'll think ahead and set up NAVAIDs in advance.

- I'll complete tasks, appropriate for the phase of flight, without getting distracted from the job of flying the airplane.

- When necessary, I'll slow down the aircraft to give me more time to complete required tasks.

32. You've had a busy business trip, with 18 IFR IAPs in the past three days. On this IAP, you break out of the clouds at 1,500 feet AGL to find a blanket of snow completely covering the ground and runway at Tiny City Airport. What will you do?

Your answer must discuss risk factors and possible mitigations, and should include the soft-field landing procedure for your aircraft.

I would attempt to mitigate the risk factors associated with this landing by:

- Attempting to call UNICOM to see if the attendant can tell me how deep the snow is.

- Considering a low approach over the runway to see what I can see and look for possible drifts or snow banks.

- Calling ATC to inquire about runway conditions at nearby airports for a possible diversion.

- Giving myself plenty of time to evaluate alternatives and set up the airplane properly. I would not hesitate to fly out of my way to where runway and services are better.

Continued

- If I proceed with landing at Tiny City Airport, I would follow the soft-field landing procedure for my aircraft. This includes keeping the nose wheel off the ground as long as possible, and minimizing braking.

This scenario reveals insufficient preflight planning. By making a phone call to the FBO to learn about local airport conditions before takeoff, I could have avoided this situation. Perhaps the reason for this poor planning is my fatigue—I've flown a lot in the past three days. Did I pass the "I'M SAFE" checklist?

33. Give me a few examples of situations that might result in a CFIT accident?

Your answer must show an understanding of controlled flight into the ground and how it occurs.

Controlled flight into terrain (CFIT) could result from situations such as:

- When the pilot descends below published minimums on an approach.
- When the pilot does not follow the prescribed Obstacle Departure Procedure.
- When the pilot does not perceive a change in terrain height and initiate a suitable climb.
- When the pilot becomes distracted and loses situational awareness.

Practical Test Checklists

Appendix 1

Applicant's Practical Test Checklist

Appointment with Examiner _____

Examiner's Name _____

Location _____

Date/Time _____

Acceptable Aircraft

Aircraft Documents

___ Airworthiness Certificate

___ Registration Certificate

___ Rating Limitations

Aircraft Maintenance Records

___ Logbook Record of Airworthiness Inspections and AD Compliance

___ Pilot's Operating Handbook, FAA-Approved Airplane Flight Manual

___ Current Weight and Balance Data

Personal Equipment

___ View-Limiting Device

___ Current Aeronautical Charts

___ Computer and Plotter

___ Flight Plan Form

___ Flight Logs

___ Current AIM, Airport Facility Directory, and Appropriate Publications

Personal Records

___ Identification—Photo/Signature ID

___ Pilot Certificate

___ Current and Appropriate Medical Certificate

___ Completed FAA Form 8710-1, Airman Certificate and/or Rating Application with Instructor's Signature (if applicable)

___ Airman Knowledge Test Report

___ Pilot Logbook with Appropriate Instructor Endorsements

___ Notice of Disapproval (if applicable)

___ Approved School Graduation Certificate (if applicable)

___ Examiner's Fee (if applicable)

Examiner's Practical Test Checklist

Applicant's Name _____

Location _____

Date/Time _____

I. Preflight Preparation

      A. Pilot Qualifications

____ B. Weather Information

____ C. Cross-Country Flight Planning

II. Preflight Procedures

____ A. Aircraft Systems Related to IFR Operations

____ B. Aircraft Flight Instruments and Navigation Equipment

____ C. Instrument Cockpit Check

III. Air Traffic Control Clearances and Procedures

____ A. Air Traffic Control Clearances

____ B. Compliance with Departure, En Route, and Arrival Procedures and Clearances

____ C. Holding Procedures

IV. Flight By Reference to Instruments

____ A. Basic Instrument Flight Maneuvers

____ B. Recovery from Unusual Flight Attitudes

V. Navigation Systems

____ Intercepting and Tracking Navigational Systems and DME Arcs

VI. Instrument Approach Procedures

____ A. Nonprecision Approach (NPA)

____ B. Precision Approach (PA)

____ C. Missed Approach

____ D. Circling Approach

____ E. Landing from a Straight-in or Circling Approach

Continued

VII. Emergency Operations

____ A. Loss of Communications

____ B. One Engine Inoperative During Straight-and-Level Flight and Turns (Multiengine Airplane)

____ C. One Engine Inoperative—Instrument Approach (Multiengine Airplane)

____ D. Loss of Primary Flight Instrument Indicators

VIII. Postflight Procedures

____Checking Instruments and Equipment

Certified Flight Instructor Supplement   Appendix 2

Certified Flight Instructor–Instrument Airplane Supplement

This CFII appendix has been designed for use in conjunction with the material presented in Chapters 1–4 of this guide, for one comprehensive outline and reference. A review of this guide should provide the CFII applicant with aid for preparation and accomplishment of the Flight Instructor Instrument Airplane practical check. This appendix may be supplemented with other study materials as noted in parentheses after each question.

A. Flight by Reference to Instruments

1. Define basic attitude instrument flying. (FAA-H-8083-15)

Attitude instrument flying may be defined as the control of an aircraft's spatial position by using instruments rather than outside visual references.

2. What are the two basic methods for learning attitude instrument flying? (FAA-H-8083-15)

The two basic methods used for learning attitude instrument flying are "control and performance" and "primary and supporting." Both methods involve the use of the same instruments, and both use the same responses for attitude control. They differ in their reliance on the attitude indicator and interpretation of other instruments.

3. Explain the control and performance method of attitude instrument flying. (FAA-H-8083-15)

Aircraft performance is achieved by controlling the aircraft attitude and power (angle of attack and thrust to drag relationship). Aircraft attitude is the relationship of its longitudinal and lateral axes to the Earth's horizon. An aircraft is flown in instrument flight by controlling the attitude and power, as necessary, to produce the desired performance. This is known as the control and performance method of attitude instrument flying and can be applied to any basic instrument maneuver. The three general categories of instruments are control, performance, and navigation instruments.

4. What are the control instruments? (FAA-H-8083-15)

The control instruments display immediate attitude and power indications and are calibrated to permit attitude and power adjustments in precise amounts. In this discussion, the term "power" is used in place of the more technically correct term "thrust or drag relationship." Control is determined by reference to the attitude indicator and power indicators. These power indicators vary with aircraft and may include manifold pressure, tachometers, fuel flow, etc.

5. What are the performance instruments? (FAA-H-8083-15)

The performance instruments indicate the aircraft's actual performance. Performance is determined by reference to the altimeter, airspeed, or vertical speed indicator (VSI).

6. What are the navigation instruments? (FAA-H-8083-15)

The navigation instruments indicate the position of the aircraft in relation to a selected navigation facility or fix. This group of instruments includes various types of course indicators, range indicators, glideslope indicators, and bearing pointers. Technologically advanced aircraft can provide all of these instruments and GPS in one electronic display, giving the pilot more accurate positional information.

7. What are the procedural steps used in the control and performance method of attitude instrument flying? (FAA-H-8083-15)

Establish an attitude and power setting on the control instruments that will result in the desired performance. Known or computed attitude changes and approximate power settings will help to reduce the pilot's workload.

Trim until control pressures are neutralized. Trimming for hands-off flight is essential for smooth, precise aircraft control. It allows pilots to divert their attention to other cockpit duties with minimum deviation from the desired attitude.

Cross-check the performance instruments to determine if the established attitude or power setting is providing the desired performance. The cross-check involves both seeing and interpreting. If a deviation is noted, determine the magnitude and direction of adjustment required to achieve the desired performance.

Adjust the attitude or power setting on the control instruments as necessary.

8. How is attitude control accomplished? (FAA-H-8083-15)

Proper control of aircraft attitude is the result of maintaining a constant attitude, knowing when and how much to change the attitude, and smoothly changing the attitude a precise amount. Aircraft attitude control is accomplished by properly using the attitude indicator. The attitude reference provides an immediate, direct, and corresponding indication of any change in aircraft pitch or bank attitude.

9. How is pitch control accomplished? (FAA-H-8083-15)

Pitch changes are made by changing the "pitch attitude" of the miniature aircraft or fuselage dot by precise amounts in relation to the horizon. These changes are measured in degrees or fractions thereof, or bar widths depending upon the type of attitude reference. The amount of deviation from the desired performance will determine the magnitude of the correction.

10. How is bank control accomplished? (FAA-H-8083-15)

Bank changes are made by changing the "bank attitude" or bank pointers by precise amounts in relation to the bank scale. The bank scale is normally graduated at 0°, 10°, 20°, 30°, 60°, and 90° and may be located at the top or bottom of the attitude reference. Normally, use a bank angle that approximates the degrees to turn, not to exceed 30°.

11. How is power control accomplished? (FAA-H-8083-15)

Proper power control results from the ability to smoothly establish or maintain desired airspeeds in coordination with attitude changes. Power changes are made by throttle adjustments and reference to the power indicators. Power indicators are not affected by such factors as turbulence, improper trim, or inadvertent control pressures. Therefore, in most aircraft little attention is required to ensure the power setting remains constant. From experience in an aircraft, you know approximately how far to move the throttles to change the power a given amount. Therefore, you can make power changes primarily by throttle movement and then cross-check the indicators to establish a more precise setting. The key is to avoid fixating on the indicators while setting the power. A knowledge of approximate power settings for various flight configurations will help you avoid overcontrolling power.

12. Explain the primary and supporting method of attitude instrument flying.

For any maneuver or condition of flight, the pitch, bank, and power control requirements are most clearly indicated by certain key instruments. The instruments that provide the most pertinent and essential information will be referred to as primary instruments. Supporting instruments back up and supplement the information shown on the primary instruments.

13. What instruments are used to determine and control pitch? (FAA-H-8083-15)

Attitude indicator, altimeter, airspeed indicator, and vertical speed indicator. The attitude indicator displays a direct indication of the aircraft's pitch attitude while the other pitch attitude control instruments indirectly indicate the pitch attitude of the aircraft.

14. What instruments are used to determine and control bank? (FAA-H-8083-15)

Attitude indicator, heading indicator, magnetic compass, and turn coordinator.

15. What instruments are used to determine and control power? (FAA-H-8083-15)

The airspeed indicator and engine instruments, which are the manifold pressure gauge (MP) and tachometer/RPM.

16. What instruments are used for trim control? (FAA-H-8083-15)

Attitude indicator, airspeed indicator, turn coordinator, and heading indicator.

17. What are the two fundamental flight skills that must be developed during attitude instrument training? (FAA-H-8083-15)

These two skills are instrument cross-check and instrument interpretation, and use of both result in positive aircraft control. Although these skills are learned separately and in deliberate sequence, a measure of proficiency in precision flying is the ability to integrate these skills into unified, smooth, positive control responses to maintain any prescribed flight path.

18. What does the first fundamental skill of instrument cross-checking consist of? (FAA-H-8083-15)

Cross-checking is the continuous and logical observation of instruments for attitude and performance information. In attitude instrument flying, the pilot maintains an attitude by reference to instruments that will produce the desired result in performance. Due to human error, instrument error, and airplane performance differences in various atmospheric and loading conditions, it is impossible to establish an attitude and have performance remain constant for a long period of time. These variables make it necessary for the pilot to constantly check the instruments and make appropriate changes in airplane attitude.

19. What are some of the common cross-check errors students make? (FAA-H-8083-15)

Fixation—staring at a single instrument; may be related to difficulties with one or both of the other fundamental skills. Student may be fixating because of uncertainty about reading the heading indicator (interpretation), or because of inconsistency in rolling out of turns (control).

Omission of an instrument from their cross-check; may be caused by failure to anticipate significant instrument indications following attitude changes.

Emphasis on a single instrument, instead of on the combination of instruments necessary for attitude information; student naturally tends to rely on the instrument they understand most readily, even when it provides erroneous or inadequate information. Reliance on a single instrument is poor technique.

20. What does the second fundamental skill of instrument interpretation consist of? (FAA-H-8083-15)

The second fundamental skill, instrument interpretation, requires the most thorough study and analysis. You must understand each instrument's construction and operating principles. Then you must apply this knowledge to the performance of the aircraft you are flying, the particular maneuvers to be executed, the cross-check and control techniques applicable to that aircraft, and the flight conditions in which you are operating.

21. What are the four components of aircraft control? (FAA-H-8083-15)

Pitch control—controlling the rotation of the aircraft about the lateral axis by movement of the elevators. After interpreting the pitch attitude from the proper flight instruments, you exert control pressures to effect the desired pitch attitude with reference to the horizon.

Bank control—controlling the angle made by the wing and the horizon. After interpreting the bank attitude from the appropriate instruments, you exert the necessary pressures to move the ailerons and roll the aircraft about the longitudinal axis.

Power control—used when interpretation of the flight instruments indicates a need for a change in thrust.

Trim—used to relieve all control pressures held after a desired attitude has been attained. An improperly trimmed aircraft requires constant control pressures, produces tension, distracts your attention from cross-checking, and contributes to abrupt and erratic attitude control. The pressures you feel on the controls must be those you apply while controlling a planned change in aircraft attitude, not pressures held because you let the aircraft control you.

22. Are there any differences in the method you would use to scan the instruments in an aircraft equipped with a primary flight display? (FAA-H-8083-6)

The PFD is not intended to change the fundamental way in which you scan your instruments during attitude instrument flying. The PFD supports the same familiar control and performance, or primary and supporting methods you use with conventional flight instruments. However, you need to train your eyes to find and interpret these instruments in their new formats and locations.

B. Instrument Certification Regulations

1. What conditions must exist for an instrument instructor, conducting a flight lesson, to log instrument time? (14 CFR 61.51)

An authorized instructor may log instrument flight time when conducting instrument flight instruction in actual instrument flight conditions.

2. What time is considered "training" time and how should this be logged? (14 CFR 61.51)

a. A person may log training time when that person receives training from an authorized instructor in an aircraft, flight simulator, or flight training device.

b. The training time must be logged in a logbook and must be endorsed in a legible manner by the authorized instructor; and include a description of the training given, the length of the training lesson, and the authorized instructor's signature, certificate number, and certificate expiration date.

3. **Concerning instructional flights with both an authorized flight instructor and a certified pilot on board, which person is allowed to log pilot-in-command time?** (14 CFR 61.51)

Both the CFII and private pilot will log PIC time. Provided the private pilot is sole manipulator of the controls of an aircraft for which the pilot is rated, that pilot may log the time as PIC.

4. **For the purposes of meeting the recent instrument experience requirements, what information must be recorded in the person's logbook?** (14 CFR 61.51)

a. The location and type of each instrument approach accomplished; and

b. The name of the safety pilot, if required.

5. **What does an instrument proficiency check consist of?** (14 CFR 61.57)

An instrument proficiency check (IPC) consists of the areas of operation and instrument tasks required in the instrument rating practical test standards. A useful table has been included in the "Introduction" section of the Instrument Rating PTS (FAA-S-8081-4)—a Rating Task Table with "IPC" as one of the columns. As a minimum, the applicant must demonstrate the ability to perform the Tasks as listed in the table. Conducting an IPC in accordance with the PTS is required.

6. **Who can give an instrument proficiency check?** (14 CFR 61.57)

14 CFR §61.57 states that the instrument proficiency check must be given by—

a. An examiner;

b. A person authorized by the U.S. Armed Forces to conduct instrument flight tests, provided the person being tested is a member of the U.S. Armed Forces;

c. A company check pilot who is authorized to conduct instrument flight tests under Part 121, 125, or 135, and provided that both the check pilot and the pilot being tested are employees of that operator;

d. An authorized instructor; or

e. A person approved by the Administrator to conduct instrument practical tests.

7. **The instrument proficiency check required by 14 CFR §61.57 can be accomplished by flying with an authorized flight instructor. Does that CFI have to be a CFII?** (14 CFR 61.193 and 61.195; AC 61-98)

The CFI should possess an instrument rating on their flight instructor certificate. The CFI should also possess an instrument rating and meet currency requirements on their pilot certificate. The basis for these are found in 14 CFR §§61.193(g) and 61.195(d) (6). For example, a comprehensive IPC in a multiengine airplane includes demonstration of engine-out procedures, which requires a CFI who holds both multiengine and instrument ratings on his or her pilot certificate.

Note: In addition to having the appropriate instructor ratings, the CFI should consider other factors relating to his or her ability to conduct an IPC. These include the factors discussed for the flight review as well as the instructor's own instrument currency.

8. **Can the instrument proficiency check be given in a flight training device or flight simulator?** (AC 61-98)

A CFI may conduct part or all of the IPC in an approved ground trainer or level-3-or-below flight training device (FTD) that meets the requirements of 14 CFR §61.4. If given in an aircraft training device, that trainer must receive specific approval for such use, in writing, by the FAA Administrator. Pilots or CFIs contemplating use of such a device for an IPC should contact their local FSDO. Guidance on the applicability of specific devices to particular tasks is located in the current edition of the Instrument Rating PTS (FAA-S-8081-4), Appendix 2, and the specific device approval document.

9. **What are several pre-check considerations a CFI should give thought to prior to conducting an IPC?** (AC 61-98)

The CFI should structure an instrument proficiency check in a manner similar to that of the flight review, tailoring the check to the needs of the pilot, reaching mutual agreement on the scope of the check, and developing a plan for accomplishing it. The CFI should develop a plan of action that uses realistic scenarios to organize and sequence the required tasks and maneuvers. The CFI and pilot should discuss the operating conditions under which the check will be conducted. If the check is conducted in an airplane, the check may be under VFR or IFR in simulated instrument conditions, or it may be under IFR in actual instrument conditions. If the check is conducted under IFR, whether conditions are simulated or actual, the CFI should ensure that the aircraft meets all Part 91 requirements for operating under IFR. Additionally, if the pilot receiving the check is no longer current under IFR, the CFI should be aware that he or she will be the pilot-in-command during the flight and must meet IFR currency requirements. The CFI should also discuss crewmember roles and responsibilities with the pilot.

10. **What standards shall be used to determine satisfactory completion of the IPC?** (14 CFR 61.57; AC 61-98)

14 CFR Part 61, section 61.57(d), sets forth the requirements for an instrument proficiency check. The person giving that check shall use the standards and procedures contained in the Instrument Rating PTS when administering the check. A representative number of tasks, as determined by the instructor, must be selected to assure the competence of the applicant to operate in the IFR environment. As a minimum, the applicant must demonstrate the ability to perform the tasks as listed in the Instrument Rating PTS Ratings Task Table for an IPC.

11. What areas of knowledge should be reviewed by the CFI when conducting the knowledge portion of an IPC? (AC 61-98)

The CFI should determine that the pilot has adequate knowledge and understanding of 14 CFR Part 91, especially Subpart B, "Instrument Flight Rules"; Subpart C, "Equipment, Instrument, and Certificate Requirements"; and Subpart E, "Maintenance, Preventive Maintenance, and Alterations." Additionally, the CFI should determine that the pilot has adequate knowledge and under standing of the following areas:

a. Instrument enroute and approach chart interpretation, including departure procedures (SIDs and ODPs), standard terminal arrival routes (STAR), and area navigation (RNAV)/global positioning system (GPS)/wide area augmentation system (WAAS) procedures.

b. Obtaining and analyzing weather information, including knowledge of hazardous weather phenomena.

c. Preflight planning, including aircraft performance, Notices to Airmen (NOTAM) information (including temporary flight restrictions [TFR]), fuel requirements, alternate requirements, and use of appropriate FAA publications such as the *Airport/ Facility Directory.*

d. Aircraft systems related to IFR operations, including appropriate operating methods, limitations, and emergency procedures due to equipment failure.

e. Aircraft flight instruments and navigation equipment, including characteristics, limitations, operating techniques, and emergency procedures due to malfunction or failure, such as lost communications procedures.

f. Determining the airworthiness status of the aircraft for instrument flight, including required inspections and documents.

g. Air Traffic Control (ATC) procedures pertinent to flight under IFR with emphasis on elements of ATC clearances and pilot/ controller responsibilities.

12. After conducting the knowledge portion of an IPC, what actions should the CFI request the pilot to complete prior to conducting the flight skill portion of the check? (AC 61-98)

The CFI should ask the pilot to prepare for the skill portion of the proficiency check by completing the necessary flight planning, obtaining current weather data, filing a flight plan, and conducting the preflight inspection. In order to fully evaluate the pilot's skills under normal operating conditions, the CFI may wish to have the pilot conduct a short IFR cross-country flight with at least part of the flight conducted "in the system" under IFR.

13. What are some of the general considerations a CFI should have in determining the specific maneuvers and procedures for an IPC? (14 CFR 61.57, AC 61-98)

The maneuvers and procedures selected for the IPC must include those listed in the Rating Task Table in the Instrument Rating PTS (FAA-S-8081-4). The CFI conducting the IPC has the discretion to require any other maneuver(s) necessary to determine that the pilot can safely operate under IFR in a broad range of conditions appropriate to the aircraft flown and the ATC environment selected. However, in any case, the CFI should pay particular attention to those areas within the PTS identified as "Special Emphasis." The CFI should emphasize proper adherence to ATC clearances. Regardless of the maneuvers and procedures selected, the CFI should ensure that the pilot demonstrates satisfactory basic attitude instrument flying skills.

14. What postflight actions and logbook entries should occur upon completion of an IPC? (AC 61-98)

Upon completion of the proficiency check, the CFI should complete the plan and checklist (if used) and debrief the pilot on the results of the check (satisfactory or unsatisfactory). Regardless of the determination, the CFI should provide the pilot with a comprehensive analysis of his or her performance, including suggestions for improving any weak areas. If the proficiency check was unsatisfactory, the CFI should not endorse the pilot's logbook, but should sign the logbook to record the instruction given. If the proficiency check was satisfactory, the endorsement for a satisfactory proficiency check should be in accordance with the current issue of AC 61-65. If a lesson plan and checklist was used, the CFI may wish to retain the plan as a record of the scope and content of the competency check, even though not required.

15. **What are the general requirements for a person to be eligible for an instrument rating?** (14 CFR 61.65)

a. Hold at least a current private pilot certificate, or be concurrently applying for a private pilot certificate, with an airplane, helicopter, or powered-lift rating appropriate to the instrument rating sought;

b. Be able to read, speak, write, and understand the English language. If the applicant is unable to meet any of these requirements due to a medical condition, the Administrator may place such operating limitations on the applicant's pilot certificate as are necessary for the safe operation of the aircraft;

c. Receive and log ground training from an authorized instructor or accomplish a home-study course of training on the aeronautical knowledge areas that apply to the instrument rating sought;

d. Receive a logbook or training record endorsement from an authorized instructor certifying that the person is prepared to take the required knowledge test;

e. Receive and log training on the areas of operation from an authorized instructor in an aircraft, flight simulator, or flight training device that represents an airplane, helicopter, or powered-lift appropriate to the instrument rating sought;

f. Receive a logbook or training record endorsement from an authorized instructor certifying that the person is prepared to take the required practical test;

g. Pass the required knowledge test on the aeronautical knowledge; however, an applicant is not required to take another knowledge test when that person already holds an instrument rating; and

h. Pass the required practical test on the areas of operation in an airplane, helicopter, or powered-lift appropriate to the rating sought; or a flight simulator or a flight training device appropriate to the rating sought and for the specific maneuver or instrument approach procedure performed. If an approved flight training device is used for the practical test, the instrument approach procedures conducted in that flight training device are limited to one precision and one nonprecision approach, provided the flight training device is approved for the procedure performed.

16. What are the aeronautical knowledge requirements for a person to be eligible for an instrument rating? (14 CFR 61.65)

A person who applies for an instrument rating must have received and logged ground training from an authorized instructor or accomplished a home-study course on the following aeronautical knowledge areas that apply to the instrument rating sought:

a. Federal Aviation Regulations that apply to flight operations under IFR;

b. Appropriate information that applies to IFR operations in the *Aeronautical Information Manual*;

c. Air traffic control system and procedures for instrument flight operations;

d. IFR navigation and approaches by use of navigation systems;

e. Use of IFR en route and instrument approach procedure charts;

f. Procurement and use of aviation weather reports and forecasts and the elements of forecasting weather trends based on that information and personal observation of weather conditions;

g. Safe and efficient operation of aircraft under instrument flight rules and conditions;

h. Recognition of critical weather situations and windshear avoidance;

i. Aeronautical decision making and judgment; and

j. Crew resource management, including crew communication and coordination.

17. What are the flight proficiency requirements for a person to be eligible for an instrument rating? (14 CFR 61.65)

A person who applies for an instrument rating must receive and log training from an authorized instructor in an aircraft, or in a flight simulator or flight training device that includes the following areas of operation:

a. Preflight preparation;

b. Preflight procedures;

c. Air traffic control clearances and procedures;

d. Flight by reference to instruments;

e. Navigation systems;

f. Instrument approach procedures;

g. Emergency operations; and

h. Postflight procedures.

18. What are the aeronautical experience requirements for a person to be eligible for an instrument rating? (14 CFR 61.65)

A person who applies for an instrument–airplane rating must have logged the following:

a. 50 hours of cross-country flight time* as PIC, of which 10 hours must have been in an airplane.

b. 40 hours of actual or simulated instrument time in the Part 61 areas of operation, of which 15 hours must have been received from an authorized instructor who holds an instrument airplane rating, and the instrument time includes:

- 3 hours of instrument flight training from an authorized instructor in an airplane that is appropriate to the instrument–airplane rating within 2 calendar months before the date of the practical test;

- Instrument flight training on cross-country flight procedures, including one cross-country flight in an airplane with an authorized instructor, that is performed under IFR, when a flight plan has been filed with an air traffic control facility, and that involves a flight of 250 NM along airways or ATC-directed routing, an instrument approach at each airport, and 3 different kinds of approaches with the use of navigation systems.

Note: An applicant for a combined private pilot certificate with an instrument–airplane rating may satisfy the cross-country flight time requirements by crediting up to 45 hours of cross-country flight time performing the duties of pilot in command with an authorized instructor.

19. What regulations apply if flight simulators or flight training devices are used for some of the training required for the instrument rating? (14 CFR 61.65)

If the instrument time was provided by an authorized instructor in a flight simulator or flight training device:

a. A maximum of 30 hours may be performed in that flight simulator or flight training device if the instrument time was completed in accordance with 14 CFR Part 142; or

b. A maximum of 20 hours may be performed in that flight simulator or flight training device if the instrument time was not completed in accordance with 14 CFR Part 142.

c. A maximum of 10 hours of instrument time received in an aviation training device (FAA approved and authorized) may be credited for the instrument time requirements of 14 CFR Part 61.

20. What is the minimum length of time a flight instructor is required to retain a record of their flight instruction activity? (14 CFR 61.189)

Each flight instructor must retain the records required by 14 CFR Part 61 for at least 3 years.

21. What are the required records a flight instructor must retain? (14 CFR 61.189)

A flight instructor must maintain a record in a logbook or a separate document that contains the following:

a. The name of each person whose logbook or student pilot certificate that instructor has endorsed for solo flight privileges, and the date of the endorsement; and

b. The name of each person that instructor has endorsed for a knowledge test or practical test, and the record shall also indicate the kind of test, the date, and the results.

22. What qualifications must a flight instructor possess before instruction may be given for the issuance of an instrument rating? (14 CFR 61.195)

A flight instructor who provides instrument training for the issuance of an instrument rating, a type rating not limited to VFR, or the instrument training required for commercial pilot and airline transport pilot certificates, must hold an instrument rating on his or her pilot certificate and flight instructor certificate that is appropriate to the category and class of aircraft used for the training he or she is providing.

23. Can a CFII give instrument instruction in a multi-engine airplane if the instructor does not possess a multi-engine instructor rating or a multi-engine rating on his/her pilot certificate? (14 CFR 61.195)

No. A flight instructor who provides instrument training for the issuance of an instrument rating, a type rating not limited to VFR, or the instrument training required for commercial pilot and airline transport pilot certificates, must hold an instrument rating on his or her pilot certificate and flight instructor certificate that is appropriate to the category and class of aircraft used for the training he or she is providing.

C. Logbook Entries Related to Instrument Certification

1. What advisory circular contains recommended sample endorsements for use by authorized instructors when endorsing airmen pilot logbooks? (AC 61-65)

AC 61-65E— *Certification: Pilots and Flight and Ground Instructors*

2. Each instructor endorsement should include what information? (AC 61-65)

Each endorsement should include—

a. Instructor signature
b. Date of signature
c. CFI certificate number
d. Certificate expiration date

3. Give examples of the endorsements you would use when endorsing a logbook for a pilot applying for an instrument rating. (AC 61-65)

Aeronautical knowledge test: §§61.35(a)(1) and 61.65(a), (b)
I certify that (First name, MI, Last name) has received the required training of §61.65(b). I have determined that he/she is prepared for the (name the knowledge test).

/s/   [date]   J.J. Jones   987654321CFI   Exp. 12-31-05

Flight proficiency/practical test: §61.65(a)(6)
I certify that (First name, MI, Last name) has received the required training of §61.65(c) and (d). I have determined he/she is prepared for the Instrument—(Airplane, Helicopter, or Powered-lift) practical test.

/s/   [date]   J. J. Jones   987654321CFI   Exp. 12-31-05

4. **Give an example of the endorsement you would use for a pilot who has just completed an instrument proficiency check.** (AC 61-65)

I certify that (First name, MI, Last name), (pilot certificate), (certificate number), has satisfactorily completed the instrument proficiency check of §61.57(d) in a (list make and model of aircraft) on (date).

/s/   [date]   J. J. Jones   987654321CFI   Exp. 12-31-05

D. Fundamentals of Instructing

1. **Briefly define the term "learning."** (FAA-H-8083-9)

Learning can be defined as a change in behavior as a result of experience.

2. **What are the basic characteristics of learning?** (FAA-H-8083-9)

Learning is:

Purposeful—Each student is a unique individual whose past experience affects readiness to learn and understanding of the requirements involved. Students have fairly definite ideas about what they want to do and achieve.

Experience—Learning is an individual process from individual experience. Previous experience conditions a person to respond to some things and to ignore others. Knowledge cannot be poured into the student's head.

Multifaceted—It may include verbal elements, conceptual elements, perceptual elements, emotional elements, and problem-solving elements all taking place at once.

Active process—Students do not soak up knowledge like a sponge absorbs water. For students to learn, they must react and respond—perhaps outwardly, perhaps only inwardly, emotionally, or intellectually.

3. What are the laws of learning? (FAA-H-8083-9)

These are rules and principles that generally apply to the learning process. The first three are the basic laws; the last three laws are the result of experimental studies.

The law of readiness—individuals learn best when they are ready to learn, and they do not learn if they see no reason for learning.

The law of exercise—those things most often repeated are best remembered. It is the basis of practice and drill.

The law of effect—learning is strengthened when accompanied by a pleasant or satisfying feeling, and that learning is weakened when associated with an unpleasant feeling.

The law of primacy—the state of being first, often creates a strong, almost unshakable, impression. What is taught must be right the first time.

The law of intensity—a vivid, dramatic, or exciting learning experience teaches more than a routine or boring experience.

The law of recency—the things most recently learned are best remembered.

4. How do people learn? (FAA-H-8083-9)

All learning involves the following:

Perception—Initially all learning comes from perceptions that are directed to the brain by one or more of the five senses (sight, hearing, touch, smell and taste).

Insight—The grouping of perceptions into meaningful wholes.

Motivation—The most dominant force governing the student's progress and ability to learn.

5. What are the factors that affect perception? (FAA-H-8083-9)

Both internal and external factors affect an individual's ability to perceive:

Physical organism—provides individuals with the perceptual apparatus for sensing the world around them; the ability to see, hear, feel, and respond.

Goals and values—every experience and sensation, which is funneled into one's central nervous system, is colored by the individual's own beliefs and value structures.

Self-concept—a student's self-image, described in such terms as "confident" or "insecure," has a great influence on the total perceptual process.

Time and opportunity—learning some things depends on other perceptions, which have preceded those learnings, and on the availability of time to sense and relate those new things to the earlier perceptions.

Element of threat—confronted with threat, students tend to limit their attention to the threatening object or condition. Fear adversely affects perception by narrowing the perceptual field.

6. What are the four levels of learning? (FAA-H-8083-9)

Rote learning—The ability to repeat back something that one has been taught, without understanding or being able to apply what has been learned.

Understanding—What has been taught.

Application—Achieving the skill to apply what has been learned and to perform correctly.

Correlation—Associating what has been learned, understood, and applied with previous or subsequent learning; this level is the overall objective of aviation instruction.

7. **Why do individuals forget what has been learned?**
(FAA-H-8083-9)

Several theories on why people forget exist, including:

Fading—a person forgets information that is not used for an extended period of time.

Interference—people forget because a certain experience has overshadowed it or the learning of similar things has intervened.

Repression or suppression—a memory is pushed out of reach because the individual does not want to remember feelings associated with it.

Retrieval failure—the inability to retrieve information.

8. **What actions can the instructor take to assist individuals in remembering what has been learned?**
(FAA-H-8083-9)

Praise stimulates remembering; responses that give a pleasurable return tend to be repeated.

Recall is prompted by association. Each bit of information or action that is associated with something to be learned tends to facilitate its later recall by the student.

Favorable attitudes aid retention; people learn and remember only what they wish to know. Without motivation there is little chance for recall.

Learning with all our senses is most effective. Although we generally receive what we learn through the eyes and ears, other senses also contribute to most perceptions.

Meaningful repetition aids recall; each repetition gives the student an opportunity to gain a clearer and more accurate perception of the subject to be learned, but mere repetition does not guarantee retention.

9. **What are "defense mechanisms"?** (FAA-H-8083-9)

Certain behavior patterns are called defense mechanisms because they are subconscious defenses against the realities of unpleasant situations.

10. What are several common defense mechanisms? (FAA-H-8083-9)

Repression—a person places uncomfortable thoughts into inaccessible areas of the unconscious mind.

Denial—a refusal to accept external reality because it is too threatening.

Compensation—a process of psychologically counterbalancing perceived weaknesses by emphasizing strength in other areas.

Projection—an individual places his or her own unacceptable impulses onto someone else.

Rationalization—a subconscious technique for justifying actions that otherwise would be unacceptable.

Reaction formation—a person fakes a belief opposite to the true belief because the true belief causes anxiety.

Fantasy—occurs when a student engages in daydreams about how things should be rather than doing anything about how things are.

Displacement—results in an unconscious shift of emotion, affect, or desire from the original object to a more acceptable, less threatening substitute.

11. How can an instructor minimize student frustrations during training? (FAA-H-8083-9)

a. *Motivate students*—more can be gained from wanting to learn than from being forced to learn.

b. *Keep students informed*—telling students what is expected of them and what they can expect in return.

c. *Approach students as individuals*—each individual has a unique personality.

d. *Give credit when due*—praise and credit from the instructor provides incentive to do better.

e. *Criticize constructively*—it is important to identify mistakes and failures and explain how to correct them.

f. *Be consistent*—the instructor's philosophy and actions must be consistent.

g. *Admit errors*—no one, including students, expects an instructor to be perfect.

12. What are the basic steps involved in the teaching process? (FAA-H-8083-9)

The teaching of new material can be broken down into the steps of:

Preparation—consists of determining the scope of the lesson, the objectives, and the goals to be attained, and ensuring the necessary supplies are available.

Presentation—consists of delivering information or demonstrating the skills that make up the lesson. The delivery could be the lecture method, guided discussion method, demonstration-performance method, etc.

Application—the student performs the procedure or demonstrates the knowledge required in the lesson.

Review and evaluation—consists of a review of all material and an evaluation of the student performance.

13. What are the three most common teaching methods? (FAA-H-8083-9)

a. Lecture method

b. Guided discussion method

c. Demonstration/performance method

14. Discuss the "lecture" method of teaching. (FAA-H-8083-9)

The lecture is used primarily to introduce students to a new subject, but it is also a valuable method for summarizing ideas, showing relationships between theory and practice, and re-emphasizing main points.

15. What is the "guided discussion" method of teaching? (FAA-H-8083-9)

In contrast to the lecture method, where the instructor provides information, the guided discussion method relies on the students to provide ideas, experiences, opinions, and information. Through the skillful use of "lead-off" type questions, the instructor "draws out" what the student knows, rather than spending the class period telling them.

16. What is the "demonstration/performance" method of teaching? (FAA-H-8083-9)

This method of teaching is based on the simple, yet sound principle that we learn by doing.

17. What are the five essential phases of the demonstration/performance method of teaching? (FAA-H-8083-9)

a. Explanation

b. Demonstration

c. Student performance

d. Instructor supervision

e. Evaluation

18. What are the three main steps involved when organizing the material for a particular lesson? (FAA-H-8083-9)

a. Introduction

b. Development

c. Conclusion

19. The "introduction" step should contain which basic elements? (FAA-H-8083-9)

Attention—gain the student's attention and focus it on the subject involved.

Motivation—should appeal to each student personally and accentuate his or her desire to learn.

Overview—tells the student what is to be covered; a clear concise presentation of the objectives and key ideas; provides a road map of the route to be followed.

20. Discuss the "development" step of a presentation. (FAA-H-8083-9)

This is the main part of the lesson. The instructor develops the subject matter in a manner that helps the student achieve desired learning outcomes. The instructor must logically organize the material to show the relationships of the main points.

21. Define the term "integrated flight instruction." (FAA-H-8083-9)

Integrated flight instruction is flight instruction during which students are taught to perform flight maneuvers both by outside references and by reference to flight instruments, from the first time each maneuver is introduced.

22. What are the general characteristics of an effective assessment? (FAA-H-8083-9)

An assessment should be:

Objective—An effective critique is focused on student performance and should not reflect the personal opinions, likes, dislikes, and biases of the instructor.

Flexible—An instructor must fit the tone, technique, and content of the critique to the occasion and the student.

Acceptable—Before students willingly accept their instructor's criticism, they must first accept the instructor. Effective critiques are presented with authority, conviction, sincerity, and from a position of recognizable competence.

Comprehensive—Effective critiques will cover a few major points or a few minor points as well as cover the overall strengths and weaknesses of the student.

Constructive—The instructor should provide positive guidance for correcting the faults and strengthening the weaknesses.

Well organized—Unless a critique follows some pattern of organization, a series of valid comments may lose their impact.

Thoughtful—An instructor should always be thoughtful towards the student's need for self-esteem, recognition, and approval from others.

Specific—The instructor's comments and recommendations should be specific, not so general that the student can find nothing to hold on to.

23. **Control of human behavior involves understanding human needs. Name the six basic needs.** (FAA-H-8083-9)

   a. Physiological

   b. Security

   c. Belonging

   d. Esteem

   e. Cognitive and Aesthetic

   f. Self-Actualization

24. **What are the basic steps in planning a course of learning?** (FAA-H-8083-9)

   Before any important instruction can begin, the following must be considered:

   a. Determination of standards and objectives.

   b. Development and assembly of blocks of learning.

   c. Identification of the blocks of learning.

25. **What is a training syllabus?** (FAA-H-8083-9)

   A training syllabus is an outline of the course of training. It uses a step-by-step, building block progression of learning, with provisions for regular review and evaluations at prescribed stages of learning. The syllabus defines the unit of training, states objectives as to what the student is expected to accomplish during the unit, shows an organized plan for instruction, and dictates the evaluation process for either the unit or stages of learning.

26. **What is a lesson plan?** (FAA-H-8083-9)

   A lesson plan is an organized outline or "blueprint" for a single instructional period and should be prepared in written form for each ground school and flight period. It should—

   a. Tell what to do

   b. What order to do it in

   c. What procedure to use in teaching it

27. What items will a lesson plan always contain? (FAA-H-8083-9)

a. Lesson objective

b. Elements included

c. Schedule

d. Equipment

e. Instructor's actions

f. Student's actions

g. Completion standards

28. Describe the steps necessary in preparing a lesson plan. (FAA-H-8083-9)

a. Determine the objective of the lesson.

b. Research the subject as defined by the objective.

c. Determine the method of instruction and lesson plan format.

d. Decide on how to organize the lesson and select suitable supporting material.

e. Assemble training aids.

f. Write the lesson plan outline.

E. Preflight Lesson on a Maneuver to be Performed in Flight

An FAA examiner will determine that the applicant exhibits instructional knowledge of the elements related to the planning of instructional activity. This will be accomplished by requiring the applicant to develop a lesson plan for any one of the required maneuvers. The following is an example of a lesson plan for a 90 minute instructional flight period.

Date _____

Lesson _____

Straight-and-Level Flight by Student _____

Reference to Instruments

Objective

To determine that the pilot:

1. Exhibits adequate knowledge of the elements related to attitude instrument flying during straight-and-level flight.
2. Maintains straight-and-level flight in the configuration specified by the examiner.
3. Maintains the heading within 10 degrees, altitude within 100 feet (30 meters), and airspeed within 10 knots.
4. Uses proper instrument cross check and interpretation, and applies the appropriate pitch, bank, power, and trim corrections.

Elements

1. Instrument cross-check
2. Instrument interpretation
3. Aircraft control (pitch, bank, power, and trim)

Schedule

1. Preflight—discuss lesson objective   :20
2. Inflight instructor demonstration   :20
3. Inflight student practice   :25
4. Postflight critique   :15
5. Assignment next lesson   :10

Equipment

1. Instrument panel mockup
2. Chalkboard/notebook
3. View limiting device
4. *Instrument Flying Handbook*

Instructor's Actions

1. Discuss lesson objective
2. Discuss concept of attitude instrument flying
3. Present straight-and-level flight on mockup from standpoint of pitch, bank, power, and trim
4. Inflight—Demonstrate straight-and-level flight by reference to instruments
5. Inflight—Direct student practice of straight-and-level flight by reference to instruments
6. Postflight—Critique student performance
7. Make reading assignments for next lesson

Student's Actions

1. Discuss lesson objective
2. Listen, take notes, ask pertinent questions
3. Inflight—Observe instructor demonstration of straight-and-level flight by reference to instruments
4. Inflight—Practice of straight-and-level flight by reference to instruments
5. Postflight—Ask appropriate questions
6. Obtain reading assignments for next lesson

Completion

The student should demonstrate that they have an understanding of the concept of attitude instrument flying and of the performance of straight-and-level flight by reference to instruments.

Common Errors

1. Slow or improper cross-check during straight-and-level flight
2. Improper power control
3. Failure to make smooth, precise corrections, as required
4. Uncoordinated use of controls
5. Improper trim control

FAA Instrument Proficiency Check Guidance

Appendix 3

The following is an excerpt from the FAA's Instrument Proficiency Check (IPC) Guidance document found at **www.faasafety.gov**. Visit **www.asa2fly.com/reader/oegi** to download the complete document, which includes additional information and helpful worksheets for both the CFII and IPC applicant.

Instrument Proficiency Check Guidance

Introduction

The certificated flight instructor (CFI) performs one of the most vital and influential roles in aviation, because the aviation educator's work matters not just for the individual pilot, but for every passenger who entrusts his or her life to that pilot's knowledge, skill, and judgment.

The instrument flight instructor—the so-called "double-eye"—carries an even greater responsibility. Weather is still the factor most likely to result in aviation accidents with fatalities. Notwithstanding the common reminder that the instrument rating is not an "all weather license," the CFI-I's endorsement for instrument privileges attests that the pilot has the knowledge and skill to operate safely in instrument meteorological conditions (IMC) during all phases of flight.

Two special challenges arise for the CFI-I who administers the instrument proficiency check (IPC) described in 14 CFR §61.57(d). The CFI-I who trains a pilot for the initial instrument rating can develop a comprehensive picture of that pilot's instrument flying knowledge, skills, and judgment, usually in an aircraft familiar to both the CFI-I and the trainee. By contrast, an IPC more often requires short-term evaluation of an unknown pilot, possibly with the added challenge of an unfamiliar aircraft and/or avionics, particularly in technically advanced aircraft. In addition, the IPC is not always conducted in the "real-world" IMC flying environment.

To ensure that the IPC serves the purpose for which it was intended, the current version of the Practical Test Standards for the instrument rating (FAA-S-8081-4) stipulates that the flight portion of an IPC must include a representative number of tasks, as determined by the examiner/instructor, to assure the competence of the applicant to operate in the IFR environment. This guide offers additional (optional) guidance, with special emphasis on conducting a thorough ground review and on administering IPCs in aircraft with advanced avionics. The goal is to help the CFI-I determine that a pilot seeking an IPC endorsement has both the knowledge and skills for safe operation in all aspects of instrument flying.

Step 1: Preparation

Expectations: Regulations for the flight review (14 CFR §61.56) require a minimum of one hour of ground training and one hour of flight training. While 14 CFR §61.57(d) does not stipulate a minimum time requirement for the IPC, a good rule of thumb is to plan at least 90 minutes of ground time and at least two hours of flight time for a solid evaluation of the pilot's instrument flying knowledge and skills. Depending on the pilot's level of instrument experience and currency, you may want to plan on two or more separate sessions to complete an IPC. For pilots with little or no recent instrument flying experience, it is a good idea to schedule an initial session in an appropriate aircraft training device (ATD).

Regulatory Review: The regulations (14 CFR §61.57[d]) state that an IPC shall consist of the areas of operation and instrument tasks required in the instrument rating practical test standards. A thorough IPC should cover general operating and flight rules for IFR as set out in 14 CFR Part 91 and in the *Aeronautical Information Manual* (AIM). To make the best use of ground time, ask the pilot to review the *Instrument Procedures Handbook* (FAA-H-8261-1), *Instrument Flying Handbook* (FAA-H-8083-15), and *Aviation Weather* and *Weather Services* in advance of your session. Remind the pilot to bring current copies of documents such as the instrument rating PTS, FAR/AIM, charts (en route and instrument approach procedures), *Airport/Facility Directory* (A/FD), and Pilot's Operating Handbook (POH) or Airplane Flight Manual (AFM) for the aircraft to be used.

As part of the IPC preparation process, you may want to ask the pilot to complete the IPC Prep Course available in the Aviation Learning Center at **www.faasafety.gov**. This online course lets the pilot review material at his or her own pace and focus attention on areas of particular interest.

Cross-Country Flight Plan Assignment: Because IFR flying is almost always for transportation purposes, structuring the IPC as an IFR cross-country—ideally one representative of the pilot's typical IFR flying—is an excellent way to evaluate real world instrument flying skills. The airport(s) to be used should have published instrument approach procedures. The flight plan should include consideration of all preflight planning elements required by 14 CFR §91.103, as well as appropriate instrument departure, arrival, and approach procedures. It should be based on a standard weather briefing for the day of the discussion and flight. If the ground and flight portions take place on different days, the pilot should have current weather for each session.

To ensure a thorough evaluation of the pilot's weather interpretation and analysis skills—especially if the weather for the actual IPC is MVFR or better—your own advance preparation might include obtaining a weather briefing for the assigned route on an IFR or low IFR (LIFR) day. You can either provide this IFR briefing to the pilot for advance analysis, or present it during the session for an on-the-spot review and evaluation.

Step 2: Ground Review

Knowledge is key to safe instrument operation, but it needs to be much deeper than the ability to recite rules and regulations. Scenario-based training is a very effective way to test a pilot's knowledge in the context of real-world IFR flying, so consider using the pre-assigned XC flight plan as a basis for both the ground review and the actual flight. A good ground review technique is to work through rules and "real world" procedures related to each phase of flight from departure to the destination airport. Topics to cover include the following:

Preflight (14 CFR §91.103)

For a flight under IFR, the pilot must become familiar with "all available information." For the pre-assigned flight plan, the pilot should be able to address the following topics:

Weather (standard briefing)

- **Describe** weather for departure, en route, and arrival, to include discussion of forecast convective activity or freezing levels/cloud bases along the intended route. For example: "Conditions for departure are VFR, but we will encounter MVFR and IFR conditions en route. Conditions for ETA at destination are IFR. There is no convective activity in the forecast, but the freezing level is expected to be just above the filed altitude."
- **Evaluate** current/forecast weather in terms of:
  - Personal minimums
  - Aircraft equipment
  - Terrain/obstacle avoidance
  - Distance, time, and fuel to nearest VFR conditions

Expected performance and equipment required (airworthiness)

- **Determine** that aircraft is appropriately equipped for proposed flight (14 CFR §§91.205(d), 91.171, Kinds of Operations Equipment List (KOEL) if provided in the Aircraft Flight Manual (AFM)).
- **Calculate** expected aircraft performance (takeoff/landing distances and cruise performance) under known and forecast conditions.
- **Describe** operation and failure modes of installed equipment (e.g., GPS, autopilot, avionics), and appropriate pilot response (including the requirement to report failures to ATC).

Alternatives

- **Determine** if weather requires filing an alternate and, if so:
- **Designate** alternates that are not only "legal," but also appropriate to conditions, pilot experience, needs, etc. If planning to fly a GPS approach to the destination, consider the need to have a non-GPS approach at the alternate unless there is a WAAS-capable GPS. Can the pilot identify viable alternatives for every 25–30 nm along the route? Does he or she establish "tripwire" conditions related to personal minimums as triggers for diversion?

Length/lighting of runways to be used

- **Determine** that available runway length is at least 150% of values shown in the POH/AFM, or at least 200% of the POH/AFM numbers for a wet, icy, or otherwise contaminated runway.
- **Explain** LAHSO procedures (AIM 4-3-11), if in effect at the airport(s) to be used.
- **Describe** expected lighting, including lighting as it applies to descent below MDA or DA (14 CFR §91.175).

Traffic delays

- **Determine** whether traffic delays might require holding, and
- **Describe** holding procedures (AIM 5-3-8). During this part of the review, you may want to give the pilot a practice holding clearance and have him or her explain how the entry would be made from the en route heading to the holding fix. For aircraft equipped with GPS moving map navigators, does the pilot understand how to set up and use this equipment to fly a non-published ("random") holding pattern?

How much fuel is required

- **Calculate** fuel requirements sufficient to fly approaches at both the destination and alternate, and
- **Decide** on the amount of reserve fuel (e.g., legal reserve plus safety margin appropriate to reported and forecast weather conditions).

Risk Management and Personal Minimums

The ground discussion should include all risk factors that affect the planned flight, as well as the types of trips the pilot typically flies. The PAVE checklist is one way to make a structured identification and analysis. For example:

Pilot: general health, physical/mental/emotional state; proficiency, currency

Aircraft: airworthiness, equipment, performance capability

enVironment: weather hazards, terrain, airports/runways to be used, conditions

External pressures: meetings, people waiting at destination, etc.

For each risk factor identified, ask the pilot what strategies can be used to mitigate or eliminate the hazards. This part of the IPC also offers an excellent opportunity to discuss personal minimums, and to help the pilot complete a personal minimums worksheet if he or she has never done so.

Personal Minimums Checklist: One of the most important concepts to convey is that safe pilots understand the difference between what is "legal" in terms of the regulations, and what is "smart" or "safe" in terms of pilot experience and proficiency. For this reason, assistance in completing a Personal Minimums Checklist tailored to the pilot's individual circumstances is perhaps the single most important "take-away" item you can offer. Use the Personal Minimums Development Worksheet in Appendix 3 to help the pilot work through some of the questions that should be considered in establishing "hard" personal minimums, as well as in preflight and in-flight decision-making for flight under IFR.

It may also be helpful to include key findings from accident data. For example, instrument pilots should be aware that non-precision approaches have an accident rate five times greater than precision approaches. Circling approaches, particularly at night, also increase risk, so the pilot should consider such factors as how much of a tailwind can be acceptable in lieu of a circling approach.

Taxi, Takeoff and Departure

Even at a familiar airport, departure under instrument meteorological conditions can be challenging. Topics to cover in this part of the review include:

Taxi Procedures and Runway Incursion Avoidance

One of the FAA's top priorities is to reduce the frequency of runway incursions and the risk of a runway collision, so be sure that the pilot can correctly identify airport markings. Give the pilot a practice taxi clearance from ramp to runway, and ask him or her to show you on the airport diagram how to execute it. If the airports to be used have only a single runway, give the pilot taxi instructions for a more complex airport.

The FAA's Runway Safety Office (**www.faa.gov/airports/ runway_safety/**) offers links to a number of resources available to help pilots operate safely on the airport surface. Sections 4-3-18 and 4-3-19 of the *Aeronautical Information Manual* (AIM) also offer guidance on safe taxi procedures, including taxi during low-visibility conditions.

Instrument Departures (AIM 5-2-8)

All departure procedures (DPs) provide a way to depart the airport and transition safely to the en route structure, but proficient instrument pilots need to understand the difference between obstacle departure procedures (ODPs) and standard instrument departure procedures (SIDs). If the airport to be used has a SID, ask the pilot to explain how he or she would file and fly that specific procedure. Other questions to ask:

Obstacle Departure Procedures:

• What is an ODP, and where do you find it?
• What functions does the ODP serve?
• Do you need an ATC clearance to fly an ODP?
• Can ATC assign an ODP for departure from a non-towered airport?
• When should you fly an ODP?
• When departing from an airport without an ODP or SID, how will you ensure terrain/obstacle clearance until reaching a published MEA?

Standard Instrument Departure Procedures:

- What is a SID, and where do you find it?
- What functions does the SID serve?
- Can you fly a SID without ATC clearance?
- How do you file a SID (e.g., how is it stated in the flight plan)?

En Route

Topics to review in connection with en route IFR operations include the following:

Airways and Route Systems

Using the proposed route of flight on the appropriate IFR en route chart, ask the pilot to talk you through the journey. Be sure that the pilot is familiar with standard terms and symbols (e.g., MEA, MOCA, MORA, COP). Most pilots are familiar with the airway system defined by VOR facilities, but if your client flies with area navigation (RNAV) equipment, be sure to review the material in AIM 5-3-4 and AIM 5-1-8(d) on RNAV routes. Questions to ask:

- What is a published RNAV (Q) route, and who can use it?
- What is an "unpublished" RNAV route, and when can you fly it?
- What is the Magnetic Reference Bearing (MRB), and what are the limitations on its use?

En Route Navigation (AIM 1-1-18)

This portion of the ground review should focus on use of the specific navigational equipment installed in the aircraft to be used for the IPC. For IPCs in aircraft equipped with GPS moving map navigators, special emphasis topics include:

- What requirements must your GPS meet before you can use it for IFR (e.g., equipment/installation approvals; operation in accordance with approved AFM or flight manual supplement, etc.).
- Under what conditions can you use GPS in place of ADF or DME equipment?
- Under what circumstances must you have (and use) means of navigation other than GPS?
- What is RAIM, and when is it required?
- What are GPS NOTAMs (1-1-18), and how do you find them?

- Must your database be current?
- How and where are GPS database updates logged?
- How does course and distance information on a GPS navigation display differ from data presented on navigational charts and conventional instrumentation?

En Route Weather

Since weather is at the heart of IFR flying, no IPC ground review can be complete without ensuring that the pilot is thoroughly familiar with sources of inflight weather information. A competent instrument pilot should know how to contact, address, and use the En Route Flight Advisory Service. As described in AIM 7-1-5, EFAS, or "Flight Watch," is a service specifically designed to provide timely, meaningful, and pertinent weather, as well as to collect and distribute pilot reports (PIREPs). EFAS is available on 122.0 between 5,000 MSL and 17,500 MSL; frequencies for other altitudes are listed in the AIM. Pilots should also be familiar with AIM 7-1-14 on ATC Inflight Weather Avoidance Assistance, including ATC descriptive terminology for convective activity and weather radar echoes. Be sure to note that there have been recent changes to the terminology that ATC uses to describe weather radar echoes.

Whether via approved installation or a portable handheld unit, weather datalink (AIM 7-1-11) provides both textual and graphical information that can help improve pilot situational awareness. While datalink has significant potential to improve GA safety, realization of these safety benefits depends heavily upon the pilot's understanding of the specific system's capabilities and limitations. With datalink, IFR pilots should pay particular attention to such system limitations as:

- *Latency.* Where would you find the time stamp or "valid until" time on the particular datalink weather information displayed in the cockpit? (*Note:* since initial processing and transmission of NEXRAD data can take several minutes, pilots should assume that datalink weather information will always be a minimum of seven to eight minutes older than shown on the time stamp and use datalink weather radar images for broad strategic avoidance of adverse weather.)

- *Coverage.* What coverage limitations are associated with the type of datalink network being used? (For example, ground-based systems that require a line-of-sight may have relatively limited coverage below 5,000 feet AGL. Satellite-based datalink weather systems can have limitations stemming from whether the network is in geosynchronous orbit or low earth orbit (LEO). Also, National Weather Service coverage has numerous gaps, especially in the western states.)

- *Content/format.* Since service providers often refine or enhance datalink products for cockpit display, pilots must be familiar with the content, format, and meaning of symbols and displays in the specific system.

Abnormal Procedures and Emergencies

An IPC ground review of abnormal/emergency procedures for IFR operations should include the following topics:

- *Loss of two-way radio communications* (AIM 6-4-1): As stated in the AIM, a pilot who experiences a radio communications failure in VFR conditions should remain VFR and land as soon as practicable. In IFR conditions, the pilot should continue via the route assigned, vectored, expected, filed and at the highest of the following altitudes or flight levels for the route segment being flown: MEA, assigned, expected. Be sure to review the AIM guidance on clearance limits.

- *Loss of avionics/equipment* (AIM 5-3-3; 14 CFR §§91.185, 91.187): Any loss of navigational capability (e.g., loss of one VOR in a dual VOR installation) during operations in controlled airspace should be reported to ATC, along with information on the degree to which the problem affects the aircraft's ability to operate under IFR in the ATC system.

- *Loss of PFD/MFD/Autopilot:* Many pilots today operate with the situational awareness advantage of moving map navigators, "glass cockpit" avionics, and capable autopilots. If your client uses such equipment, or if it is installed in the aircraft to be used for the IPC, have the pilot describe failure modes and recommended procedures for each piece of equipment. The pilot should also be able to describe how one failure may affect other installed components (e.g., how would failure of the AHRS or ADC affect the autopilot?).

Arrival and Approach Procedures

Check for the pilot's understanding of the ways to fly an instrument approach:

- Via pilot navigation ("own nav"):
  - Where are the IAFs?
  - Which IAFs require a course reversal, and how should it be flown?
- Via vectors
  - What are minimum vectoring altitudes?
  - How can you maintain position awareness relative to nearby terrain?
- Via direct to IF (intermediate fix)
  - Is a course reversal required if a racetrack is depicted at the IF?
  - What are the requirements for a controller to issue a clearance direct to the IF?

Standard Terminal Arrival Procedures (AIM 5-4-1)

In reviewing the basics of flying a standard terminal arrival procedure (STAR), points to cover include the following:

- How do you file a STAR?
- When navigating a STAR, when may you descend?
- What does it mean if ATC instructs you to "descend via" the STAR?
- Do you need the approved chart in order to fly a STAR?
- What is an RNAV STAR?

Terminal Arrival Areas (AIM 5-4-5)

Some pilots may not be familiar with the concept of terminal arrival areas, which have been designed to provide a seamless transition from the en route structure to the terminal environment for aircraft equipped with GPS or Flight Management System (FMS) navigational equipment. Questions to ask:

- How are TAA lateral boundaries identified?
- How can the pilot determine which area of the TAA the aircraft will enter?
- When ATC clears you to enter the TAA, what are you expected to do?

Instrument Approach Procedures (AIM 5-4-5)

In addition to reviewing the terms, symbols, and basic steps for flying a conventional instrument approach procedure (e.g., ILS, LOC, VOR, NDB), you will also want to see whether the pilot understands RNAV (GPS) procedures and charting formats, with special emphasis on the minimums section. For example:

- What is LPV?
  - How do you know if you can fly to LPV minimums?
  - Does it include a DA or MDA?
  - At what point does the missed approach begin?
- What is LNAV/VNAV?
  - How do you know if you can fly to LNAV/VNAV minimums?
  - Does it include a DA or MDA?
  - What limitations (e.g., temperature) apply if using a WAAS receiver?
  - Can you use a remote altimeter setting with a WAAS receiver?
- What is LNAV+V?
  - At what point does the vertical glide path intercept the MDA?
- What is LNAV?
  - How do you know if you can fly to LNAV minimums?
  - Does it include a DA or MDA?

Another area to cover is the use of visual descent points (VDPs), which are described in AIM 5-4-5. For example:

- What is a VDP?
  - How is the VDP identified on the chart?
  - What techniques are required to fly a procedure with a VDP?
  - If the approach includes a VDP, when may you descend below MDA?

Missed Approach Procedures

Missed Approach (AIM 5-4-21 and AIM 5-5-5)

The missed approach procedure (MAP) is one of the most challenging maneuvers a pilot can face, especially when operating alone (single pilot) in IMC. Safely executing the MAP requires a precise and disciplined transition that involves not only aeronautical knowledge and skill—the natural areas of focus in most training programs—but also a crucial psychological shift. There is little room for error on instrument missed approach procedures, and a pilot who hesitates due to deficits in procedural knowledge, aircraft control, or mindset can quickly come to grief. Important MAP topics to cover in the IPC ground review include:

- At what point must you execute the MAP:
  - When flying a precision approach?
  - When flying a non-precision approach?
- What is the proper procedure if the decision to miss is made prior to reaching the MAP?
- Do rules and procedures require you to fly to the filed alternate after a missed approach at the intended destination?
- After executing the missed approach, what factors should you consider when deciding whether to make a second attempt, as opposed to proceeding to an alternate?

Step 3: Flight Activities

A proficient instrument pilot must possess knowledge and skill in three distinct, but interrelated, areas:

- *Aircraft control skills* (i.e., basic attitude instrument flying, or (BAI)—crosscheck (including effective scan), interpret, and control. If the pilot flies in "glass cockpit" aircraft, the discussion should include appropriate and effective scanning techniques for these aircraft.
- *Aircraft systems knowledge* (i.e., knowledge and proficiency in instrument procedures and aircraft systems, including GPS/FMS, autopilot, datalink);
- *Aeronautical decision-making (ADM) skills* (i.e., higher-order thinking skills, flight planning and flight management, cockpit organization, weather analysis/anticipation).

There may be a temptation to focus the flight portion of the IPC on the first of these three areas (aircraft control), and to proceed sequentially through the required items chart in the PTS (FAA-S-8081-4). While these activities can provide a snapshot of the pilot's aircraft control skills, a series of approaches and other maneuvers conducted "out of context" will tell you little about the pilot's knowledge of avionics and other aircraft systems, and even less about the pilot's ability to make safe and appropriate decisions in real-world instrument flying.

Having the pilot fly the cross-country trip you assigned and discussed in the ground review is a good way to make a more thorough and integrated assessment of the pilot's knowledge, skills, and judgment. Since ATC procedures are a critical part of instrument flying, ask the pilot to file and fly one leg "in the system." A leg that involves flying from departure to destination gives you an opportunity to evaluate the pilot's communication skills, systems knowledge and day-to-day decision-making skills, including risk management.

The other leg (which can come first, depending on how you choose to organize the exercise) can focus more on basic attitude instrument (BAI) flying, approaches, and holding patterns. For example, you might fly the return leg of the cross-country under VFR, putting the pilot under the hood for BAI exercises. At some point, give the pilot a scenario that requires a diversion (e.g., mechanical problem, unexpected weather below minimums). Ask the pilot to choose an alternate destination and, using all available and appropriate resources (e.g, chart, basic rules of thumb, "nearest" and "direct to" functions on the GPS) to calculate the approximate course, heading, distance, time, and fuel required to reach the new destination. Proceed to that point and, if feasible, do some of the basic aircraft control work (approaches, including circling approach, missed approach, and holding) at the unexpected alternate.

The diversion exercise has several benefits. First, it generates "teachable moments," which refers to those times when the learner is most aware of the need for certain information or skills, and therefore most receptive to learning what you want to teach. Diverting to an airport surrounded by high terrain, for example, provides a "teachable moment" on the importance of obstacle awareness and terrain avoidance planning. Second, the diversion exercise quickly and efficiently reveals the pilot's level of skill in each of the three areas:

- *Aircraft control skills:* The PTS task chart requires one precision approach and one non-precision approach, plus loss of primary flight instruments. Does the pilot maintain control of the aircraft when faced with a major distraction, and/or when flying the missed approach procedure? Consider as well asking the pilot to remove the hood and land out of a practice approach to DA or MDA. For a satisfactory IPC, the pilot should be able to perform all maneuvers in accordance with the Practical Test Standards (PTS) for the pilot certificate that he or she holds. If the pilot is flying a multi-engine aircraft for the check, a single-engine approach is essential.

- *Aircraft systems knowledge:* Does the pilot demonstrate knowledge and proficiency in using avionics and aircraft systems, including GPS moving map navigators and the autopilot? The pilot should be thoroughly familiar with both normal and abnormal operation of all systems, and understand how they work together in IFR flying. In technically advanced aircraft, does the pilot understand the significance of indicators for "ENR," "TERM," and "APR?" Does the pilot correctly manage the sequence for selecting navigation source and arming the autopilot's approach mode? Does the pilot effectively access and manage the information available in onboard databases?

- *Aeronautical decision-making (ADM) skills:* Give the pilot multiple opportunities to make decisions. Asking questions about those decisions is an excellent way to get the information you need to evaluate ADM skills, including risk management. For example, ask the pilot to explain why the alternate airport selected for the diversion exercise is a safe and appropriate choice. What are the possible hazards, and what can the pilot do to mitigate them? Be alert to the pilot's information and automation management skills as well. For example, does the pilot perform regular "common sense" cross-checks of what the GPS and/or the autopilot are doing? Does the pilot always keep track of position when being vectored, using cross radials? Does the pilot maintain awareness of weather, personal minimums and alternates at all times?

Step 4: Post Flight Debriefing

Most instructors have experienced the traditional model of training, in which the teacher does all the talking and hands out "grades" with little or no student input. There is a place for this kind of debriefing; however, a collaborative critique is a more effective way to determine that the pilot has not only aircraft control skills and systems knowledge, but also the situational awareness and judgment needed for sound aeronautical decision-making. Here is one way to structure a collaborative post flight critique:

Replay: Rather than starting the IPC post flight briefing with a laundry list of areas for improvement, ask the pilot to verbally *replay* the flight for you. Listen for areas where your perceptions are different, and explore why they don't match. This approach gives the pilot a chance to validate his or her own perceptions, and it gives you critical insight into his or her judgment abilities.

Reconstruct: The reconstruct stage encourages the pilot to learn by identifying the "would'a could'a should'a" elements of the flight—that is, the key things that he or she *would have, could have,* or *should have* done differently.

Reflect: Insights come from investing perceptions and experiences with meaning, which in turn requires reflection on these events. For example:

- What was the most important thing you learned today?
- What part of the session was easiest for you? What part was hardest?
- Did anything make you uncomfortable? If so, when did it occur?
- How would you assess your performance and your decisions?
- Did you perform in accordance with the Practical Test Standards?

Redirect: The final step is to help the pilot relate lessons learned in this flight to other experiences, and consider how they might help in future flights. Questions:

- How does this experience relate to previous flights?
- What might you do to mitigate a similar risk in a future flight?
- Which aspects of this experience might apply to future flights, and how?
- What personal minimums should you establish, and what additional proficiency flying and training might be useful?

Step 5: Instrument Practice Plan

Offer the pilot an opportunity to develop a personalized IFR skill maintenance and improvement plan. Such a plan should include consideration of the following elements:

Personal Minimums Checklist: As noted earlier, one of the most important concepts to convey in the flight review is that safe pilots understand the difference between what is "legal" in terms of the regulations, and what is "smart" or "safe" in terms of pilot experience and proficiency. For this reason, assistance in completing a personal minimums checklist tailored to the pilot's individual circumstances is perhaps the single most important "takeaway" item you can offer. The Personal Minimums Development Worksheet in Appendix 3 is one tool you can use to help the pilot work through issues that should be considered in establishing "hard" personal minimums, as well as in preflight and inflight decision-making.

Instrument Proficiency Practice Plan: Many pilots would appreciate your help in developing a plan for maintaining and improving basic instrument flying skills.

Training Plan: Discuss and schedule any additional training the pilot may need to achieve individual flying goals. For example, the pilot's goal might be to develop the competence and confidence needed to fly IFR at night, or to lower personal minimums in one or more areas. Use the form in Appendix 7* to document the pilot's aeronautical goals and develop a specific training plan to help him or her achieve them.

The IPC is a vital link in the general aviation safety chain. As a person authorized to conduct this review, you play a critical role in ensuring that it is a meaningful and effective tool for maintaining and enhancing GA safety.

---

* of the FAA full version—see online source reference given on Page A3-1.

References

14 CFR §61.57(d)—*Instrument proficiency check.*

Except as provided in paragraph (e) of this section, a person who has failed to meet the instrument experience requirements of paragraph (c) for more than six calendar months may reestablish instrument currency only by completing an instrument proficiency check. The instrument proficiency check must consist of the areas of operation and instrument tasks required in the instrument rating practical test standards.

(1) The instrument proficiency check must be—
    (i) In an aircraft that is appropriate to the aircraft category;
    (ii) For other than a glider, in a flight simulator or flight training device that is representative of the aircraft category; or
    (iii) For a glider, in a single-engine airplane or a glider.

(2) The instrument proficiency check must be given by—
    (i) An examiner;
    (ii) A person authorized by the U.S. Armed Forces to conduct instrument flight tests, provided the person being tested is a member of the U.S. Armed Forces;
    (iii) A company check pilot who is authorized to conduct instrument flight tests under part 121, 125, or 135 of this chapter or subpart K of part 91 of this chapter, and provided that both the check pilot and the pilot being tested are employees of that operator or fractional ownership program manager, as applicable;
    (iv) An authorized instructor; or
    (v) A person approved by the Administrator to conduct instrument practical tests.

AC 61-65E

Completion of an instrument proficiency check: §61.57(d)
I certify that (First name, MI, Last name), (pilot certificate), (certificate number), has satisfactorily completed the instrument proficiency check of §61.57(d) in a (list make and model of aircraft) on (date).

S/S   [date]   J. J. Jones   987654321CFI   Exp. 12-31-05

NOTE: No logbook entry reflecting unsatisfactory performance on an instrument proficiency check is required.

For aviation safety information and online resources, visit www.faasafety.gov

Checklist for Instrument Proficiency Check

Step 1: Preparation
- Expectations
- Regulatory Review
- Cross-Country Flight Plan Assignment

Step 2: Ground Review
- Preflight
- Taxi, Takeoff, Departure
- En route
- Arrival and Approach
- En Route
- Missed Approach

Step 3: Flight Activities
- Aircraft Control (BAI)
- Systems and Procedures
- Aeronautical Decision-Making

Step 4: Postflight Discussion
- Replay, Reflect, Reconstruct, Redirect
- Questions

Step 5: Instrument Practice Plan
- Personal Minimums Checklist
- Instrument Proficiency Practice Plan
- Training Plan (if desired)

Ground Review

Pilot

61.57	Recency of Experience
91.3	PIC responsibilities and authority
91.103	Preflight actions
AIM 8	Medical facts for pilots

Aircraft

91.167	Fuel requirements
91.171	Equipment check (VOR)
91.185	IFR two-way radio communications failure
91.187	Malfunction reports
91.205	Required instruments and equipment
91.207	ELT
91.209	Aircraft lights
91.213	Inoperative instruments and equipment
91.411	Altimeter and pitot-static system tests
91.413	ATC transponder tests

Environment

91.123	ATC instructions
91.169	IFR flight plan
91.173	ATC clearance and flight plan
91.175	TO and LDG in IFR
91.177	Minimum IFR altitudes
91.179	IFR cruising altitudes
91.181	Course to be flown
91.183	IFR two-way communications
AIM 1	Navigation aids
AIM 4	Air traffic control
AIM 5	Air traffic procedures

External Pressures

91.185	IFR two-way radio communications failure
AIM 6	Emergency procedures
AIM 5-6	National security and interception procedures

Flight Activities

Area of Operation	Date
I. Preflight Preparation	
A. Pilot Qualifications	
B. Weather Information	
C. Cross-Country Flight Planning	
II. Preflight Procedures	
A. Aircraft Systems Related to IFR Operations	
B. Aircraft Flight Instruments and Navigation Equipment	
C. Instrument Cockpit Check	
III. Air Traffic Control Clearances and Procedures	
A. Air Traffic Control Clearances	
B. Compliance with Departure, En Route, and Arrival Procedures and Clearances	
C. Holding Procedures	
IV. Flight by Reference to Instruments	
A. Basic Instrument Flight Maneuvers	
B. Recovery from Unusual Flight Attitudes	
V. Navigation Systems	
A. Intercepting/Tracking Navigational Systems and DME Arcs	
VI. Instrument Approach Procedures	
A. Nonprecision Approach (NPA)	
B. Precision Approach (PA)	
C. Missed Approach	
D. Circling Approach	
E. Landing from a Straight-in or Circling Approach	
VII. Emergency Operations	
A. Loss of Communications	
B. One Engine Inoperative During Straight-and-Level Flight and Turns (Multiengine Airplane)	
C. One Engine Inoperative—Instrument Approach (Multiengine Airplane)	
D. Approach with Loss of Primary Flight Instrument Indicators	
VIII. Postflight Procedures	
A. Checking Instruments and Equipment	

Note: Structure the flight portion as an out-and-back IFR XC, with one leg focused on XC procedures (including missed approach and diversion procedures) and the other leg focused on airwork (aircraft control).

Pilot's Instrument Experience Summary

Pilot's Name: _____ CFI: _____

Address: _____

Phone(s): _____ e-mail: _____

Type of Pilot Certificate(s):

☐ Private ☐ Commercial ☐ ATP ☐ Flight Instructor

Rating(s):

☐ Instrument ☐ Multi-engine

Experience (Pilot):

Total time _____ Last 6 months _____ Avg hours/month _____

Time logged since last IPC _____

Experience (Aircraft):

Aircraft type(s) you fly _____

_____

Aircraft used most often _____

For this aircraft:

Total time _____ Last 6 months _____ Avg hours/month _____

Experience (Flight environment):

Approximately how many hours have you logged in:

Day VFR _____ Day IFR _____ IMC _____

Night VFR _____ Night IFR _____ Approaches _____

Approaches to minimums _____ Approaches in last 6 months _____

Type of Flying (External factors):

What percentage of your flying is for:

Pleasure _____ Business _____ Local _____ XC _____

Personal Skills Assessment:

What are your strengths as a pilot? _____

What do you most want to practice/improve? _____

What are your aviation goals? _____

Notes